Fundamentals of Political Economy

Volume I

Contents

8. The Incurable Disease of Capitalism

9. The Unchanging Nature of Imperialism

10. Imperialism is the Eve of Proletarian Socialist Revolution

Introduction (by George C. Wang)

Fundamentals of Political Economy is a popular introductory economics text published in the People's Republic of China in 1974 as a part of the Youth Self-Education series designed particularly for individual or group study. The primary purpose of this series, according to the preface, is to elevate the cultural level of the youths going down to the countryside, to advance their knowledge of the social and natural sciences, as well as to arouse their class consciousness. This translation makes available a comprehensive and authentic text of the Chinese version of Marxist political economy, a version which differs profoundly from that of the Soviet Union. (1)

Fundamentals of Political Economy was originally published in two volumes. The first volume (11 chapters) is a critical review of the historical development of capitalism. The second volume (12 chapters) deals with Marxist economic principles and the manner in which they are applied in China.

Volume I is an informative historical account from a Chinese point of view and stands as a valuable primer on Marxist political economy in general. Volume II will be of particular interest to students of Marxism as it has been applied to the Chinese economy because it is the Chinese Communists, probably Mao Tse-tung more than anyone else, who first successfully applied Marxist theory to a semicolonial and semifeudal society with a predominantly agricultural economy (other than the Mongolian People's Republic). Today China's sweeping and thoroughgoing social changes, such as land reform and the socialization of the means of production, appeal to peoples in developing countries who are disappointed with the slow progress of development under capitalism.

The principal features, some of which we will discuss in more detail below, of the Chinese model of economic development outlined in Volume II may be characterized as follows:

1. The Socialization of the Means of Production (Chapters 12-15)
2. Economic Planning and Proportional Growth between Sectors (Chapter 16)

3. Agriculture Is the Foundation, and Industry Is the Leading Factor
   (Chapter 17)
4. Practicing Economy and Capital Accumulation (Chapter 18)
5. The Economic Structure by the Type of Ownership (Chapter 19)
6. National Income and Its Distribution (Chapters 20-21)
7. Foreign Trade and Foreign Aid, and the Future of Socialism
   (Chapters 22-23)

1. Socialization of the Means of Production

In the 1950s a transitory arrangement known as state-private joint operation was set up for the purpose of smoothing the transition of large (such as textiles) and middle-size enterprises (such as hardwares) that had remained in private hands in a way that would make it possible to continue the enterprises while changing the ownership system. There were two variants of joint operation — by enterprise and by trade. In the joint enterprise the state was a partner, participating in investment and management. The private shares were to be paid off by the company out of its net revenue. In manufacturing, those producing the same type of products in the same locality were organized into a "special company" under the supervision of the Industrial Bureau of the local government.

The broadening of state control over consumer goods began

in November 1953, as grains and edible oil wefe put under a scheme known as "planned purchase and planned supply." In September 1954, raw cotton and cotton cloth were brought into it as well. (2) The state set up an annual quota of procurement that had to be fulfilled under fixed procurement prices. The "planned supply" part of the scheme meant some form of rationing in accordance with availabilities, based partly on consumers' needs, and partly on the state's requirements for export and for commodity reserves. The operation of these two schemes resulted in the elimination of an open market for controlled goods, although government-controlled grain markets continued to exist.

Earlier, mainly between 1950 and 1952, lands confiscated from landlords and rich peasants were redistributed to poor peasants. But land redistribution was only a means to an end because (1) private ownership was incompatible with socialism, and (2) the landholding after the redistribution was too small to operate economically. This was especially true with regard to the large-scale capital formation necessary to raise agricultural output substantially. Initially, it was planned to make collectivization a gradual process, but the slow growth of agricultural output and the reappearance of such capitalist phenomena as speculation and increasing polarization of income led to a decision to accelerate the process. So in 1955 the CCP organized peasants into agricultural producers' cooperatives in which farm tools and draft animals were collectively owned, and land, although still privately owned, was collectively operated; the members were paid according to their work days and their land-contribution. A year later, the land too was collectivized, and the members were paid only according to their labor.

On August 29, 1958, the Party Central Committee published a directive demanding prompt merger of all producers' cooperatives into communes embracing whole townships (hsiang), each comprising about 5,000 peasant households. The institutionalizing of the commune was partly for economic reasons — such as economies of scale; partly for political reasons — such as reducing disparities between urban areas and the countryside; and partly for social reasons — such as shortening the process of transition to communism. It was meant ultimately to help smooth the transition from collective ownership to ownership by the people as a whole. (3) Thus, by the end of the 1950s the economy was virtually socialized.

2. Economic Planning

The allocation of scarce resources between alternative and competing ends in China is determined not by the interplay of the forces of supply and demand but rather by systematic planning. As Mao Tse-tung pointed out:

A constant process of readjustment through state planning is needed to deal with the contradiction between production and the needs of society. Every year our country draws up an economic plan in order to establish a proper ratio between accumulation and consumption and to achieve a balance between production and needs. (4)

In China stress has been placed on the proportional growth between the following sectors: (1) agriculture and industry, (2) the sub-sectors within agriculture, (3) the sub-sectors within industry, (4) production and transportation, (5) material production and social welfare, (6) consumption and accumulation, (7) population growth and output, and (8) various regions.

3. Agriculture Is the Foundation

In 1959 the ideological disputes between the PRC and the USSR reached their peak, and in 1960 the Soviet Union recalled all its technical advisers and canceled hundreds of contracts vital to China's industrialization. Compounded by difficulties that had developed in communes and by two consecutive years of floods and drought, and in the wake of the uneven results of the Great Leap Forward, the economy went into a period of consolidation. It was against this background that the CCP reoriented its economic policy to "taking agriculture as the foundation and industry as the leading factor." Mao pointed out:

As China is a large agricultural country with over 80 percent of her population in the rural areas, industry must develop together with agriculture, for only thus can industry secure raw materials and a market, and only thus is it possible to accumulate fairly large funds for building a powerful heavy industry. (5)

Reflecting the increased emphasis on agriculture, grain output was reported to have risen from a depressed level of 160 million tons in 1960 to 240 million tons in 1970, (6) and to 274.9 million tons in 1974. (7) If we exclude the initial period of experimentation with the new institutional forms which the Great Leap Forward established, then output rose from 180 million tons in 1962 to 274.9 million tons in 1974. (8) In his address to the National People's Congress in 1975, the late Premier Chou En-lai indicated that between 1964 and 1974 the gross value of agricultural output increased by 51 percent, while that of industrial output increased by 190 percent. (9)

4. Practicing Economy

One of the principal obstacles to economic development is the vicious cycle of low per capita income and a low rate of savings. As Mao Tse-tung pointed out, "We want to carry on large-scale construction, but our country is still very poor. One way of resolving it is to make a sustained effort to practice strict economy in every field." (10) Indeed, the ratio of saving to national income in China has risen since the 1950s. It reached as much as approximately 25 percent of national income (U) in 1958 and probably has remained well above 20 percent since then.

To practice economy, it is necessary to set up a comprehensive economic accounting system. Economic accounting is defined as: the activities of recording, calculating, and analyzing the costs accrued in the process of production or rendering productive services. (12) In his 1942 directive concerning the establishment of the economic accounting system, Mao Tse- tung called for "centralization in leadership, and decentralization in management." (13) The former means that the state would set up production targets for each state enterprise regarding quality, quantity, variety, productivity, costs, accumulations, as well as targets for profit taxes. Decentralization in management means that, given these targets or constraints, each state enterprise is responsible for its own profit and loss. As indicated in Chapter 20, profits from state enterprises constitute the main source of capital accumulation in China.

Each of the production units under the collective ownership is an independent accounting unit responsible for its own profit and loss. The collectives are constituent parts of the national planning system. They sell and purchase according to the prices set by the state.

5. The Economic Structure by the Types of Ownership

In China, there are three major types of ownership: (1) ownership by the people as a whole, (2) collective ownership, and (3) private ownership. The characteristics of economic transactions are determined by the types of ownership of the means of production. In the third type of ownership prices are determined within limits set by the state, by the supply and demand in the market. Goods exchanged according to market conditions include the products of household subsidiary activities and produce grown in private plots, both of which may be sold at trade fairs. The characteristics of the second type of ownership are that (1) the prices of the products traded are fixed by the state, (2) the transactions are not for profit. The characteristic of the third type of ownership is that all production is determined by state planning. However, since the products are treated as commodities, they are governed by the law of value in the transactions, and money is used as the medium of exchange.

State enterprises are owned by the people as a whole, and there are three types of exchanges among them. The first type of transaction is direct supply, that is, raw materials and equipment being delivered directly from the producing unit to the using unit. The second type of transaction consists of raw materials or semi-finished products being shipped to a third state enterprise for further processing or fabrication before being delivered to consumption-oriented enterprises. Another type of transaction includes various assorted small articles such as bolts, nails, and screws which can be used either in production or in consumption. In 1973, state enterprises accounted for 92.5 percent of China's retail trade, while collective enterprises accounted for 7.3 percent. (14)

6. National Income and Distribution

The concept of national income adopted by China is that of material product, net of depreciation. The product for any one year is composed of net contributions from industry, agriculture, restaurants, freight transportation, and that part of trade and communications which serves the materially productive sectors. Omitted are not only passenger transportation and private use of communications, but also finance and insurance, public administration, army and internal security, education, public health, private housing, and all other professions that render services to the people. (15)

In the state sector of the economy, national income by distributive shares, or the primary distribution, in Chinese terminology, consists of two components: (1) wages and (2) state revenue from profit and taxes. The collective sector is similar, except that a collective enterprise may retain a portion of its profits for accumulation and welfare fund.

The nonproductive sectors of the economy including educational, cultural, social welfare, and others receive their share of the national income from what is called the "second-round" distribution of national income. In effect, funds are appropriated for these activities through the state budget. To a certain extent, the distribution of national income among various sectors in a socialist economy can be carried out through adjusting the relative prices of products or factors of production.

At present, 99 percent of the state revenue in China is derived from state enterprises and the collectives. (16) Expenditures for economic, social, and cultural construction in the state budget rose from approximately 36 percent in 1960 to 70 percent in 1973. From 1949 to 1973, the value of agricultural production increased 1.8-fold; light industry, 12.8-fold; heavy industry, 59-fold; state revenue, 13-fold; and state expenditures, 11-fold.

Estimates by Western Scholars

The visit to Peking of President Nixon ushered in a new epoch in our perceptions of Chinese development. Many American economists have toured the PRC, including Professors Wassily Leontief and John Kenneth Galbriath from Harvard University; James Tobin and Lloyd G. Reynolds from Yale University; and John Gurley from Stanford. According to Tobin's estimate, the 1974 Chinese GNP in the Western concept of national accounting was approximately $145 per capita. (17) This is close to Reynolds' estimate which amounted to $150 per capita. Taken literally, this would imply imminent starvation of the population. "The error in the calculation," Reynolds explained, "arises from the fact that Chinese prices for basic consumer goods are much lower than U.S. prices; thus, the purchasing power of the yuan is much higher than the official exchange rate suggests." (18)

Professor Gurley's 1971 appraisal of the PRC's economic performance is more optimistic..... the Chinese people over the past two decades have made very remarkable economic advances (though not steadily) on almost all fronts. The basic, overriding economic fact about China is that for twenty years she has fed, clothed, and housed everyone, has kept them healthy, and has educated most. Millions have not starved; sidewalks and streets have not been covered with multitudes of sleeping, begging, hungry, and illiterate human beings; millions are not disease-ridden.... In this respect, China has outperformed every underdeveloped country in the world.... China's gains in the medical and public health fields are perhaps the most impressive of all. (19)

However, some economists are less optimistic. For instance, Professors T. C. Liu and K. C. Yeh in their estimates of China's national income from 1952 to 1959 suggested that during 1952- 57, the average annual rate of growth of net domestic product was 6 percent per year in constant 1952 prices. (20)

A. G. Ashbrook, a U.S. government expert on China, in his review of the economy sums up the 1975 outlook as follows:

...The economy of the People's Republic of China has proved an effective mechanism for supplying the minimum needs of the population, modernizing the industrial sector, and supporting a formidable defense establishment. With its floor under construction, its purposeful investment program, its control over migration to urban areas, and its hard-driven leadership, China has easily outdistanced other LCDs." (21)

Finally, Professor Victor D. Lippit, in assessing China's rapid economic growth, stressed the increase in the share of national income devoted to capital formation, an increase made compatible with rising mass consumption by the redistribution of income. He pointed out:

The experience of China in raising her national savings - investment ratio by taking advantage of the situation created when revolution forced the traditional claimants on the nation's economic surplus to relinquish their claims is perhaps the most significant in world history. (22)

Concluding Remarks

With these varying and provocative interpretations of the Chinese developmental experience, we now turn to the translation of this key Chinese text on political economy. It is here that we develop a keener sense of how the Chinese perceive, through the Maoist prism, Marxian political economy as applied to their own set of priorities and goals for national development — priorities and goals that are in some cases unique to China and in some cases shared with other developing countries.

At a time when a new, post-Mao Tse-tung, era is developing in China, when, judging at least from initial signs, there will be renewed emphasis on economic development and modernization of the means of production, we feel that Fundamental s of Political Economy provides a timely and valuable means to understanding the critical issues that are alive in China today.

A Bibliographic Note

Fundamentals of Political Economy is a translation of "Cheng-chih ching-chi hsueh chi-ch'u chih-shih", which was first published in May 1974 by the Shanghai People's Press. While this translation was in preparation, a second edition was published in December 1975. A comparison of the two printings reveals few revisions in content or in style. There are some changes however which should be mentioned.

In the first printing, the subtitle of Chapter 17, reads: "The Relations among Socialist Agriculture, Light Industry, and Heavy Industry." In the second printing it has been revised to:

"Correctly Handle the Relations between Agriculture and Industry, and Consolidate the Worker-Peasant Alliance." During the First Five-Year Plan (1953-57), first priority was accorded to heavy industry because it was believed that that would speed up industrialization. The new policy adopted at the beginning of the 1960s stated that agriculture is the foundation, and industry is the leading factor. What is the justification for such a revision? In the second printing, the authors found a justification in the Communist Manifesto, where Marx and Engels are quoted as referring to the "... combination of agriculture with manufacturing industries; gradual abolition of the distinction between town and country." (23)

In the first printing, the title of the last section of Chapter 21 was "Nurture the Communist Labor Attitude." In the second printing, it has been revised to: "Criticize Bourgeois Ideology and Advocate a Communist Labor Attitude." While both printings admit that the principle of distribution under socialism is "From each according to his ability, and to each according to his labor," the second printing contends that differentials in wage scales should not be wide; otherwise, they would dampen revolutionary enthusiasm. Moreover, it asserts that under favorable conditions, as socialist construction proceeds, efforts should be made toward the realization of "From each according to his ability, and to each according to his needs." The differences between the two versions are in stress, not in principle. Nowhere, however, is it indicated how wage scales are objectively determined. The title of Chapter 22 in the second edition has been revised to: "Mutual Aid, and Mutual Benefit on an Equal Basis." There is little revision in the content.

A final note: in virtually all cases, quotations from Western works, such as those of Marx and Engels, and quotations from Mao's works were translated here directly from the Chinese.

Notes

1) To analyze the similarities and differences of the Chinese interpretation of Marxist economic principles and those of the Soviet Union, see A. Leontief s Political Economy, A Popular Introductory Text for Individual or Group Study (International Publishers), a standard Soviet text.

2) Jen- min shou-ts'e (People's Handbook, 1955), Tientsin, pp. 456-458; Hsin Hua News Agency, October 15, 1954.

3) Edgar Snow, R ed Chin a Today (revised and updated edition of The Other Side o f the River), New York, Vintage Books, Random House, pp. 405-410.

4) Mao Tse-tung, "On the Correct Handling of Contradictions among the People," in Mao Tse-tung and Lin Piao, Post-Revolutionary Writings, edited by K. Fan, Doubleday Anchor, pp. 164-1657

5) Mao Tse-tung, "On the Correct Handling of Contradictions among the People," p. 193.

6) Alva Lewis Erisman, "China: Agriculture in the 1970s," in U.S. Congress, Joint Economic Committee, China: A Reassessment of the Economy. Washington, D.C. U.S. Government Printing Office, 1975, pp. 328-329.

7) Output figure cited by Agriculture and Forestry Vice- Minister Yang Li-kung at a Food and Agricultural Organization Conference in Rome, November 4, 1975. Reported in Current Scene, Vol. XIV, No. 1 (January 1976) p. 20.

8) Ibid.

9) The Economist Intelligence Unit, Quarterly Economic Review: Chin a, Hong Kong, North Korea,^Jo. 1, 1975, p. 3.

10) Mao Tse-tung, "On the Correct Handling of Contradictions among the People," pp. 164-165.

11) Po I-po, "The Correct Disposition of the Relationship between Accumulation and Consumption," Jen-min jih -pao (People's Daily), September 20, 1956.

12) Fundamentals of Political Economy, pp. 398-399.

13) Ibid., p. 402.

14) Ibid., p.445.

15) Yueh Wei, "The Method of Computing National Income," Ching-chi y en -chiu (Economic Research), 3: 48-66, August 1956

16) Fundamentals of Political Economy, p. 445.

17) Chinese Economic Studies, VIH: 3 (Spring 1975), pp. 25-46.

18) Ibid., pp. 8-24.

19) John G. Gurley, "Capitalist and Maoist Economic Development," Monthly Review, February 1971, pp. 15-35 and pp. 26-27.

20) Ta-chung Liu, and Kung-chia Yeh, "Economic Development in Mainland China, Preliminary Estimate of the National Income of the

Chinese Mainland, 1952-59," American Economic Review, Vol. LI, No. 2 (May 1961), pp. 489-498*.

21) Joint Economic Committee, U.S. Congress, Compendium on China, A. G. Ashbrook, Jr., "China: Economic Overview, 1975," July 10, 1975, Government Printing Office.

22) Victor D. Lippit, Land Reform and Economic Development in China: A Study of Institutional Change and Development Finance, White Plains, N.Y., M. E. Sharpe, Inc. (International Arts and Sciences Press), 1975, p. x.

23) Karl Marx and Friedrich Engels, "Manifesto of the Communist Party," in Lewis S. Feuer, ed., Marx and Engels, Basic Writings on Politics and Philosophy, New York, Doubleday and Company, 1959, p. 28.

1. Learn Some Political Economy

The Object of Political Economy

The great Chairman Mao teaches us over and over again to learn some political economy. This is not only a requirement for Communist Party members and revolutionary cadres; it is also a requirement for every combatant in the Three Great Revolutionary Struggles. To learn some political economy is very important for understanding Marxism, for penetratingly criticizing revisionism and transforming our world outlook of our own accord, and especially for a deeper appreciation of the Party's basic line and policies in the whole socialist historical stage.

The youths fighting in the front lines of the countryside and factories are our country's hope and the successors to the proletarian revolutionary enterprise. To better engage in combat, to grow healthily and more quickly, the youths must learn some political economy.

The Object of Political Economy Is Production Relations

What kind of science is political economy? We must start from its object of study. The object of study for Marxist political economy is production relations. Engels clearly pointed out that "what economics investigates is not things, but the relations among people and ultimately the relations among classes." (1) How do production relations among people arise? We must start from man's productive activities.

Chairman Mao said, "Marxists regard man's production activities as the most basic practical activities which determine all other activities." (2) But, over a hundred years ago, before Marxism was created, people did not have this scientific understanding. Thinkers of the exploiting class all opposed this viewpoint. They either championed the fallacy that human society developed according to God's will or peddled the heresy of heroes creating history. These so-called thinkers glossed over the simplest fact, namely, that people must first be able to feed, clothe, and shelter themselves before they can engage in politics, science, fine arts, and religious activities. If people need food, clothing, and shelter, they must engage in productive activities. Therefore, the direct production of material commodities forms the basis of human societal development. Without the productive activities of the laboring class, people cannot survive, and society cannot develop. It was Marx who discovered this law of development in human history.

To produce, people must form certain mutual relationships. Isolated individuals cannot engage in production. Just as Marx pointed out: "To engage in production, people form certain associations and relationships. Only within these social associations and relationships can there be a relation between them and Nature and can there be production." (3) These relations formed by people during the production process are called production relations. In class society, these relations are ultimately reflected in class relationships.

Production relations consist of three aspects: (1) the ownership pattern of the means of production; (2) people's roles in production and their mutual relations; (3) the pattern of product distribution. The ownership pattern refers to who owns the means of production (including means of labor, such as machines, plants, and land, and objects of labor, such as raw materials). In production relations, the most important aspect is the ownership pattern of the means of production. It is the basis of production relations. The ownership pattern of the means of production determines the nature of production relations. Primitive society, slave society, feudal society, capitalist society, and socialist society in human societal development are classified according to the differences in their ownership patterns of the means of production. The ownership pattern determines people's roles in production and their mutual relations and thus the distribution pattern of products.

To produce, it is necessary not only to have relations among people but also relations between man and Nature. Man must conquer and transform Nature. The power which man uses to conquer and transform Nature is called productive forces. Productive forces are composed of men and materials (namely, means of production). In productive forces, tools of production are the most important. The types of tools used for production reflect the magnitude of man's power to conquer Nature. But we cannot regard tools of production as the determining factor in productive forces. "The determining factor is man, not materials." (4) "Of all things in the world, man is the most valuable." (5) Because tools have to be used by man, created by man, and renovated by man, without man, there would be no tools and no know-how. Without man, the best "automatic" tools are never really "automatic."

Production relations and productive forces comprise the two aspects of social production. In overall historical development, productive forces are generally revealed as the major determining factor. Any transformation of production relations is necessarily a result of a certain development in productive forces. Production relations must be compatible with productive forces. When certain production relations become incompatible with the development of productive forces, these production relations must be replaced by some other new production relations which better match the development in productive forces. This is to say, the form of production relations is not determined by man's subjective will, but by the level of development of productive forces. Production relations must conform to the development of productive forces. This is an objective law which is not subject to change according to people's will. The emergence, development, and extinction of certain production relations unfold with a corresponding evolution of the contradictions of certain productive forces. Therefore, in the study of production relations, Marxist political economy also studies productive forces.

In the overall development of history, if productive forces are revealed to be the major determining factor, does it mean that production relations are entirely passive compared with productive forces? Definitely not. When production relations are compatible with productive forces, they exert an active im petus to the development of productive forces. When productioi relations become incompatible with productive forces, they wi hinder the development of productive forces. As productive forces cannot be developed without changing production relations, the transformation of production relations plays a majoi determining role. When old China was under the rule of imperialism, feudalism, and bureaucratic capitalism, the landlord and the comprador represented the most reactionary and back ward production relation of China. Productive forces were severely restricted and sabotaged. Before liberation, China did not have any machine-building industry or any automobile or airplane manufacturing. The annual output of steel was only several hundred thousand tons outside of Northeast China. Eve daily necessities were imported. Cloth was called foreign clot! umbrellas were called foreign umbrellas. Even a tiny nail was called a foreign nail. Under those circumstances, the overthrow of the rule of imperialism, feudalism, and bureaucratic capitalism, the transformation of comprador-feudal productior relations, and the establishment of socialist production relations played an important role in promoting the development of productive forces.

Big development of productive forces often occurs after the transformation of production relations. This is a universal la^ Big development of productive forces in capitalist society also occurred after the disintegration of feudal production relations induced by the bourgeois revolution and the rapid development of capitalist production relations. Take England, for example, where big development of productive forces occurred on the basis of the bourgeois revolution in the seventeenth century and the Industrial Revolution of the late eighteenth and early nineteenth centuries. The modern industries of France, Germany, the United States, and Japan rapidly developed only after the old superstructure and production relations had been transformed in various ways. On the issue of production relations and productive forces, one of the principal aspects of the long struggle between the Marxists and the Soviet revisionists has always been whether one should insist on taking the dialectical unity viewpoint or should expound the reactionary productivity- first viewpoint. Lin Piao, in league with Ch'en Po-ta, advocated that the major task after the Ninth Party Congress was to develop production. This is a copy of the revisionist fallacy inserted into the Resolution of the Eighth Party Congress by Liu Shao-ch r i and Ch'en Po-ta which pointed out "the contradiction between the advanced socialist system and the backward social productive forces." In China, socialist production relations are basically compatible with the development of the productive forces. This opens up a new horizon for the development of the productive forces. But it also has its imperfect aspects. And these imperfections contradict the development of the productive forces. The experience of socialist revolution teaches us that it is always the superior socialist system which promotes the development of the productive forces. It is always after the transformation of those parts of production relations which are incompatible with the development of the productive forces that the development of the productive forces is promoted. Where is "the contradiction between the advanced socialist system and the backward social productive forces"? The criminal intent of Liu Shao-ch'i's, Lin Piao's, and other similar swindlers' advocacy of this fallacy was to vainly attempt to use the productivity · first viewpoint as a weapon to oppose the continuing revolution under the proletarian dictatorship and the basic Party policy laid down by Chairman Mao for the socialist stage. This is their impossible dream.

Production relations must be compatible with productive forces. The development of productive forces necessitates the destruction of old production relations which are not compatible with it and their replacement by new production relations which are compatible with its development. But the process of disintegration of old production relations and the appearance of new production relations cannot be a smooth one. The transformation of old production relations and the establishment and perfection of new production relations are often realized only after revolutionary struggles. Therefore, if one wants to understand how old production relations are transformed and new production relations are established and perfected, it is not enough to explain in terms of the contradictions between production relation and productive forces. The relations between the superstructur and the economic substructure must also be investigated.

The superstructure refers to the national government, army, law, and other political systems and their corresponding ideological forms, such as philosophy, literature, and fine arts. The economic substructure is production relations. "The sum total of these production relations forms the economic substructure of society, the real basis upon which a legal and political super* structure arises and to which definite social forms of conscious ness correspond." (6) This statement by Marx scientifically explains the relation between the superstructure and the economic substructure.

In the contradiction between the superstructure and the economic substructure, the latter, in general, is the determining force.

The economic substructure determines the superstructure. Witt change in the economic substructure, "the whole immense superstructure is slowly or rapidly transformed." (7) This is to say, the old economic substructure has disintegrated, and the superstructure built upon this foundation must also disintegrate. But the rate of its disintegration varies. When reactionary state machinery has been transformed, the reactionary classes do not willingly bow out of the historical stage with the disappearance of the old economic substructure. They inevitably engage in prolonged and desperate struggle with the advanced classes in the political, ideological, and cultural spheres. In particular, old ideological forms associated with the overthrown classes remain for a long time.

The superstructure is determined by the economic substructure. Once it is established, it has an immense negative effect on the economic substructure. Stalin pointed out, "The substructure creates its superstructure to serve its own establishment and consolidation and to destroy the old substructure and its superstructure." (8) This explains why the superstructure always serves its economic substructure. The socialist superstructure serves its socialist economic substructure, and the capitalist superstructure serves its capitalist economic substructure.

In capitalist society, with the intensification of the contradictions between the socialization of production and the private ownership of means of production, there is an urgent need to replace capitalist private ownership with socialist public ownership. But the bourgeoisie controls the reactionary state machinery and uses it to maintain the capitalist economic substructure. If the proletariat does not first smash the capitalist state machinery, it is impossible to destroy the capitalist economic system. The new and old revisionists' claim that "capitalism can peacefully grow into socialism" is all a pack of lies.

In socialist society, the superstructure and the economic substructure are basically compatible. But due to the existence of the bourgeoisie and its ideological forms, some bureaucratic styles of work in the state organs, and defects in certain parts of the state system, the consolidation, perfection, and development of the socialist economic substructure was hindered or undermined. We must makethe socialist superstructure better serve the socialist economic substructure. We must firmly grasp the struggle in the superstructure and carry the socialist revolution in the superstructure to the end.

Political economy touches upon the most practical and immediate interests of various classes and strata. It explains the most acute and intense problems of class struggle. Marxist political economy, like Marxist philosophy, publicly proclaims that it is at the service of proletarian politics. Political economy is a science about class struggle.

Political Economy Is the Theoretical Basis for the Party's Defining the Basic Line

Marxist political economy was born with the appearance of the modern proletariat and the big productive forces — big industries. Marx participated in the class struggles of his time. He used revolutionary materialist dialectics to analyze the cap italist society. He revealed the secrets of how the capitalists exploited the workers and scientifically demonstrated the contradictions between the socialization of production and capitalist ownership. These contradictions were manifested as acute antagonism between the proletariat and the bourgeoisie. With the daily development of capitalist social contradictions, the proletariat, who acted as the gravediggers of the capitalist sys tern, daily strengthened. 'The knell of capitalist private property will soon be struck. The expropriators will be expropriated." (9) From this, the revolutionary and scientific conclusion of the inevitable replacement of the capitalist system by the socialist system and the bourgeois dictatorship by the proletarian dictatorship was arrived at. 'This conclusion was arrived at by Marx according to the law of economic motion in modern society." (10) Thus, Marxist political economy, along with Marxist philosophy and scientific socialism, became the theoretical basis for the proletarian political party to formulate its basic policy. On the theoretical basis of Marxism and under capitalist conditions, the proletarian revolutionary leaders formulated for the proletarian party the basic political line of using revolutionary violence to seize political power. They guided the proletariat to struggle for the complete overthrow of the bourgeoisie and all exploiting classes, the replacement of bourgeois dictatorship by proletarian dictatorship, the triumph of socialism over capitalism, and the realization of communism.

In socialist society, Marxist political economy still provides the theoretical basis for the proletarian party's formulation of basic lines. Chairman Mao has penetratingly analyzed the contradictions between socialist production relations and products forces and between the superstructure and the economic substructure and has demonstrated the long duration and complexity of class struggle and line struggle in the socialist period. On this theoretical basis, he further formulated the basic line for our Party for the entire socialist stage. This basic line tells us: "Socialist society covers a considerably long historical period. Throughout this historical period, there are classes, class contradictions, and class struggle, there is the struggle between the socialist road and the capitalist road, there is the danger of capitalist restoration, and there is the threat of subversion and aggression by imperialism and social imperialism. These contradictions can be resolved only by depending on the theory of continued revolution under the dictatorship of the proletariat and on practice under its guidance." (11) The Party's basic line guides the Chinese people to persist in continuing revolution under the proletarian dictatorship, to struggle for the consolidation of the proletarian dictatorship, the prevention of capitalist restoration, and the building of socialism, and to struggle for the great ideal of worldwide realization of communism.

The basic task of socialist political economy is to study and illustrate the law of transformation from socialist production relations to communist production relations. Some understanding of political economy helps us to understand the objective law of socialist economic motion and the inevitability of the association, distinction, and development of various production relations. This will increase our understanding of the Party's basic line and elevate our awareness about implementing it.

It is of fundamental importance to insist on the Party's basic line. It is simply "to carry out Marxism, not revisionism." To carry out Marxism, we must first learn Marxism. To oppose revisionism, we must be able to tell what revisionism is. But, Marxism consists of philosophy, political economy, and scientific socialism. If we want to understand Marxism, we must seriously study Marxist philosophy and scientific socialism, but we must also seriously study Marxist political economy. Marxist political economy is in opposition to all bourgeois and revisionist political economy, and it developed from the process of challenging bourgeois and revisionist political economy. Learning Marxist political economy helps to distinguish between Marxism and revisionism, between socialism and capitalism, and between the proletariat and the bourgeoisie. It will also correct tendencies toward deviation and elevate our ideological awareness.

In summary, we must study some political economy if we want to overcome anti-Party, anti-Marxist thinking, better carry through the Party's basic line for the socialist stage, more penetratingly unfold the criticism of Lin Piao and the rectification of the style of work, and score new and greater victories in the great socialist revolution and socialist enterprise.

Combine Theory with Practice to Learn Political Economy Well

Political economy is a demonstration and application of dialectical materialism and historical materialism. To learn political economy, we must follow the guidance of dialectical materialism and historical materialism. "The dialectical method attempts to understand every set pattern through its continuous motion and its temporary nature. It does not wor- shipanything, andit is critical and revolutionary innature." (12) This proletarian world outlook is in direct opposition to ideal-j ism and metaphysics. Only after we fully appreciate dialectical materialism and historical materialism and use them to obseH and analyze the law of motion in capitalist society and economy; can we understand why capitalism is bound to perish and social? ism will triumph. And only when we use them to observe and analyze the law of motion in socialist society and economy can we understand the duration and complexity of class struggle and line struggle in socialist society, and only then can we understand the general tendency of development from socialism to communism and why it cannot be averted by human will. This will strengthen our faith to struggle for the ultimate victory of the communist enterprise with full determination and without fear of sacrifice and difficulties.

To study political economy, we must insist on the revolutionary style of learning, which combines theory with practice. Chairman Mao teaches us:,r We must thoroughly know Marxist theory and be able to apply it. The purpose of thoroughly knowing it lies in applying it." (13) To combine theory and practice is a question of revolutionary discipline and a question of the nature of the Party. We must combine the study of political economy with the criticism of modern revisionism, with the criticism of the reactionary fallacies peddled by Liu Shao-ch'i, Lin Piao, and similar swindlers, with the Three Great Revolutionary Practices of class struggle, production struggle, and scientific experiment, and with the transformation of the world outlook. "Marxist philosophy considers that the most important question is not being able to explain the world through an understanding of the laws of the objective world, but being able to use this understanding to transform the world." (14)

Is it difficult to learn Marxist political economy? Yes. In the preface to the first edition of Capital, Marx said: "Everything starts out difficult. Every science is this way." In the concrete analysis of objective phenomena, Marxist political economy penetrates the surface, grasps the essence, and undertakes scientific abstraction. Thus, when we start, we often come across some terms and concepts which are difficult to understand. But Marxist political economy was written for the proletariat and talked about proletarian revolution. If only we seriously study it, we can understand it gradually. " T There are no difficult things, only people without sufficient resolve.* If it is not difficult to start, it is also feasible to do advanced study. All that is needed is the determination and the ability to learn." (15)

Marx once pointed out: 'There is no smooth path in science. Only those who are not afraid of climbing the steep mountain paths can expect to reach the summit of brilliance." (16) Proletarian revolutionary leaders spent their whole lives establishing and developing Marxist theory. Following their shining examples and diligently reading works by Marx, Lenin, and Chairman Mao, we should struggle to study for the mastery of this Marxist theoretical weapon, for the socialist revolution and the socialist construction enterprise, and for the worldwide realization of communism.

Major Study References

Marx, "Introduction to A Critique of Political Economy."

Engels, Anti-Dühring, Part 2, Chapter 1.

Lenin, Karl Marx ("Marx's Economic Theories").

Chairman Mao, "On Contradiction," Section 4.

Chairman Mao, "On the Correct Handling of the Contradictions among the People," Section 1.

Review Problems

1. Why is political economy a science of class struggle?
2. Why do we say that Marxist political economy is an important theoretical basis for the Party's basic line?
3. How can one learn political economy well?

Notes

1) Engels, "Karl Marx 'A Critique of Political Economy,'" Selected Works of Marx and Engels, Vol. 2, Jen-min ch'u-pan- she, 1972, p. 123.
2) "On Practice," Selected Works of Mao Tse-tung, Vol. 1, Jen-min ch'u-pan-she, 1968, p. 259.
3) Marx, Wage Labor and Capital, Selected Works of Marx and Engels, Vol. 1, Jen-min ch'u-pan-she, 1972, p. 362.
4) "On Protracted War," Selected Works of Mao Tse-tung, Vol. 2, Jen-min ch'u-pan-she, 1968, p. 437.
5) "The Bankruptcy of the Idealist Conception of History,"

Selected Works of Mao Tse-tung, Vol. 4, Jen-min ch'u-pan-she 1968, p.1401. -

6) Marx, "Introduction to A Critique of Political Economy." Selected Works of Marx and Engels, Vol. 2, Jen-min ch'u-pan- she, 1972, p. 82.

7) Ibid., p. 83.

8) Stalin, Marxism and Linguistics, Jen-min ch f u-pan-she, 1971, P- 4.

9) Marx, Capital, Vol. 1, Complete Works of Marx and Engels, Vol. 23, pp. 831-832.

10) "Karl Marx," Selected Works of Lenin, Vol. 2, Jen-min ch'u-pan-she, 1972, p. 599.

11) "Constitution of the Chinese Communist Party," Collect ed Documents from the Tenth Chinese Communist Party Congress, Jen-min ch'u-pan-she, 1973, p. 44.

12) Marx, "Epilogue to the Second Edition of Capital," Complete Works of Marx and Engels, Vol. 23, p. 24.

13) "The Rectification of the Party's Style of Work," Selected Works of Mao Tse-tung, Vol. 3, Jen-min ch'u-pan-she, 1968, p. 773.

14) "On Practice," Selected Works of Mao Tse-tung, Vol. 1, Jen-min ch'u-pan-she, 1968, p. 268.

15) "Strategic Questions in China's Revolutionary War," Selected Works of Mao Tse-tung, Vol. 1, Jen-min ch'u-pan-she, 1968, p. 165.

16) Marx, "Preface to the French Edition of Capital," Complete Works of Marx and Engels, Vol. 23, p. 26.

2. Social and Economic Systems Preceding Capitalism

Production Relations in the Primitive, Slave, and Feudal Societies

The primitive, slave, and feudal societies are the three societal systems which preceded capitalism. To comprehend the replacement and substitution of the production relations in these societies helps us to understand the historical process of the development of production relations in human society. It is especially significant for the understanding of the origin and development of capitalist production relations and the historical law governing their inevitable replacement by socialist production relations.

The Primitive Commune Established the Earliest Production Relations in Human History

Labor Created Man

The primitive society started from the separation of man from the animal world. Human societies appeared simultaneously with the emergence of man. With man, the first chapter of human history began. The history of human society is about a million years long. Man's ancestors were a kind of highly developed ape-man. How did the ape-man develop into man? The key lies in labor.

Labor began with the making of tools. In the process from ape-man to man, natural objects were transformed into suitable tools. It may only have been the striking of one stone against another to make stone knives and axes or the shaping of branches into crude tools, but a great revolution appeared. Man separated himself from the animal world and could rely on his own hands to make tools for the transformation and conquest of Nature. Just as Engels said: Labor "is the first basic condition for human life. This is true to the extent that we must, in a certain sense, admit that labor created man himself." (1) In the long process of labor, man learned how to make stone tools, hunt, and fish. He invented bows and arrows. Especially important was the discovery and use of fire. This greatly increased man's power to conquer and transform Nature. Engels highly valued this achievement. He said: "As far as worldwide liberation is concerned, the discovery of making fire through friction surpasses the importance of the invention of the steam engine.' Because the discovery of making fire through friction enabled man to control a natural force, he was thus separated from the animal world." (2) From that time on, human society made its formal appearance on this earth.

Production activities conducted after man's separation from the animal world were from the start a kind of social and group activity. "Every individual cooperated with other members of the society to form production relations to engage in production activities for the material needs of human life." (3) When the curtains of human social history were raised, the production relations were those of the primitive commune, and they were the first production relations in human history.

Clan Commune Ownership Was the Basis of the Primitive Commune Production Relations

The primary social and economic organization of the primitive society was the clan commune united on the basis of kinship for the purpose of labor. Clan commune ownership was a primitive form of collective ownership. Land and other means of production were owned by all the members of the commune. At that time, because of the crude stone knives, axes, spears, bows, and arrows used, only by collective labor could the great natural forces be conquered. Therefore, individual ownership of means of production and products was not possible. This clan commune ownership system was the only form adopted under the low level of productive forces. Means of production collectively owned by the clan commune included production tools, land, forests, rivers, and livestock. Weapons, bows, and arrows were carried and used by individuals.

In the primitive society, all able-bodied members participated in productive labor. They employed a natural division of labor based on sex and age. Men went out to hunt, old men mad tools, and women harvested plants, managed household chores, and engaged in primitive agriculture. Children helped women do auxiliary labor. Interpersonal relations were primitive cooperative relations. Under the conditions of clan commune ownership and collective labor, products were shared equally. Because of the low level of productive forces at that time, products obtained through labor were only sufficient to maintain a minimum level of subsistence with little left over. If distribution had not been equal, some members of the clan would have starved, or the clan might have disintegrated.

The economic substructure of the primitive society also produced its corresponding superstructure. The primitive society successively passed through the matriarchal and patriarchal clan stages. The formation of the matriarchal clan was the result of the more important positions occupied by women in productive activities. At that time, women were mainly occupied with primitive agriculture, and men with hunting. But hunting was more seasonal, and its results chancy. Agriculture was a more reliable source of means of livelihood. Therefore, social life revolved around the female. With the development of productive forces, agriculture advanced from its primitive form and animal husbandry was separated from agriculture. Men's importance in productive activities was elevated. With the transition from group marriages centering around women to one-to-one marriages, women's positions were rendered more subordinate, ushering in the patriarchal clan.

The clan council, composed of all the adult members of the clan, was the highest power organ in the clan commune. The clan council elected the clan chief and wartime military leaders and deliberated and decided on all important matters. [Lewis H.] Morgan, an American scholar, described in his Ancient Society the clan commune of the American Indians as follows:

"All members were free persons and were obliged to protect each other's freedom. Everybody had equal rights. Not even the clan chief and military leaders could ask for any preferential privilege. They were compatriots based on blood relations." This superstructure of the clan was instrumental in consolidating and developing the clan economic substructure and in advancing the productive forces at that time.

Chairman Mao points out: "The development of the Chinese people (here with reference mainly to the Han people) was similar to other peoples in the world. They passed through many tens of thousands of years in a classless, primitive society." (4) The society connected with the "Peking Man" which was discovered in Chou-k'ou-tien suburb of Peking represented the earliest stage of China's primitive society. Many old sites and cultural relics from primitive societies discovered in many areas of China prove that matriarchal clan tribes once existed in the central region along the Yellow River basin and extended to Inner Mongolia, Heilungkiang, Sinkiang, Tibet, Kwangsi, Szechuan, and Yunnan. About five thousand years ago, tribes along the Yellow River and Yangtze River basins gradually became patriarchal clan communes. Before the Hsia dynasty in China, the primitive society existed for several hundred thousand years.

Historical facts tell us that the primitive society had no private property, no classes, no class exploitation, or class oppression. They strongly refute the fallacy that private property and classes have been with us from time immemorial.

The Emergence of Private Property Led to the Collapse of the Primitive Commune

In the course of development in the primitive society, with the development of productive forces, social division of labor arose. In the beginning, animal husbandry was separated from agriculture. Some tribes specialized in animal husbandry. Other tribes specialized in agriculture. This was the first major social division of labor. Later on, handicraft activities were separated from agriculture. This was the second major division of labor. Toward the end of the primitive society, iron was discovered. The appearance of iron symbolized the advancement of human society to a higher stage. But it also heralded the collapse of the primitive society. With the separate appearance of agriculture, animal husbandry, and handicraft activities, production for the purpose of exchange, namely commodity production, appeared.

With the continual development of productive forces, some surplus was available after the maintenance of a basic level of subsistence. The two major divisions of labor increased labor productivity and promoted the development of agriculture, animal husbandry, and handicraft activities. Surplus products and social wealth increased. Under these conditions, the possibility of some people expropriating the labor products of other people occurred. On the other hand, with the expansion of exchange, the possibility of the clan chief gradually converting commune property into his own private property also arose. The use of metal tools — especially iron axes, iron hoes, and iron plows — markedly increased labor productivity and created conditions for production on an individual household basis. The original collective production based on the clan gradually dissolved into individual production based on the household. Production changed from a collective to a private matter. Means of production and products also became private property. Then, land formerly collectively owned but assigned to individual households also passed into private hands. Private ownership appeared and the primitive commune disintegrated.

With the emergence of private ownership, inequality in the distribution of property among families arose. The clan chiefs continuously used their power to convert collective property into their private property and became the wealthiest households in the clan. At the same time, as the wealth of these rich families increased and their scope of operation expanded, labor shortages were experienced. On the other hand, with the development of productive forces, the use of slave labor became possible and profitable. As a result, prisoners of war were no longer slaughtered but were converted into slaves. Later on, some poor people of the clan also became slaves of the rich families. The exploitation of people by people emerged.

With the development of production and the expansion of exchange, the third major division of labor occurred. There arose merchants who specialized in commodity exchange. With the development of commodity exchange, money came into being. With the appearance of money, the rich families engaged in usury and accelerated the concentration and uneven distribution of wealth. As a result, wealth rapidly became concentrated in the hands of a few slave owners. On the other hand, the broad laboring masses were forced into slavery by poverty and bankruptcy, rapidly swelling the ranks of the slaves. Thus, society was separated into classes: the slave owners and the slaves. These two opposing classes made their first appearance in human history. With the appearance of classes, the former clan council evolved from being society's public servant into being its master and became a tool by which the slave owners oppressed the slaves. The state — the machinery for the oppression of one class by another class — was born at that time. From that time up to the present, "all social history has been the history of class struggle." (5)

Slavery Was the Earliest System of Exploitation

The Characteristic of Production Relations in the Slave Society Was the Ownership of the Means of Production and of Slaves by the Slave Owner

In the slave society, the slave owner not only owned the means of production, but also slaves. The slave was merely a living tool under the absolute domination of the slave owner. The slave was not only exploited, he was treated as an animal, a sacrificial object, and a commodity. He could even be slaughtered by his owner. Slave labor was overt forced labor. The slave owner used brute force to make the slave work and indiscriminately tortured his slaves. To make it easier to catch runaway slaves, the slave owners even branded slaves and put them in fetters. The slave owner used the crudest means to extract surplus labor and products from the slave. All products produced by the slave belonged to the slave owner. The slave was fed like an animal, just enough to keep him alive. This, then, was the production relation of the slave society.

Chairman Mao points out, "About four thousand years have elapsed between the present and the time when the primitive society of the Chinese nation disintegrated into a class society, passing through the slave society and the feudal society." (6) China developed into a slave society after the Hsia dynasty. In the Yin dynasty, "chung-jen" and, "f hsu-min" ["the masses"] were all slaves. Clay burial figures unearthed in Yin-hs'u (the abandoned site of the capital of the Yin dynasty, in the vicinity of Hsiao-t'un-ts'un, An-yang, Honan Province) all had handcuffs. The male figures were cuffed with their hands behind them, and the females in front. These were reflections of slave lives at that time. The slaughter of slaves was even more hair-raising. The slave owner often sacrificed his slaves in sacrificial ceremonies. In some ceremonies during the Yin dynasty, more than a thousand people were killed. From the tombs of slave owners in the Yin dynasty, slaves were found buried alive or dead. They ranged from more than ten to several hundreds. Among them were both males and females, even children. There is no doubt that the slave society existed in China.

But, Trotskyites like Ch'en Po-ta spread the fallacy that there was no slave society in China in a vain attempt to negate the universal truth of Marxist classification of human societies and to create evidence for their fallacy that communism was not suited to Chinese conditions. This is reactionary in the extreme and utterly futile.

Class Antagonism Led to the Opposition between Urban and Rural Areas and between Mental and Physical Labor

The earliest ancient city appeared at the end of the primitive society and was established at the central region of the tribal alliance for the purpose of defense. After the formation of the slave society and with the development of agriculture, handicraft industry, and commodity exchange, the opposition between the city and the countryside arose.

At that time, industrial products were handicraft products. The city was the center of the handicraft industry. The development of the handicraft industry was related to the development of commerce.

Therefore, the city was also the center of commercial activities. In China's Yin dynasty, commerce developed rapidly. Commercial cities emerged. Yin and Shang [shang is the Chinese term for commerce] are synonymous, and the Yin dynasty is also known as the Shang dynasty. Present- day Yin-hsu was the site of a fairly large commercial city in the Yin dynasty.

The slave owner established a superstructure corresponding to the economic substructure of the slave society, and the city became the political center of the slave society. The slave owner paid special attention to strengthening the state machinery in the city to suppress the rebellion of slaves. Many slave owners, big merchants, usurers, and bureaucrats were concentrated in the city, leading evil and extravagant lives. To satisfy their needs for recreation, the slave owner forced the slaves to build beautiful palaces, temples, theaters, and other public places. The city thus gradually developed into the cultural center of the slave society.

Thus, the city in the slave society assumed a dominating economic, political, and ideological role and created opposition between the city and the countryside. The opposition between the city and the countryside was a product of acute class contradictions. It was characterized by urban exploitation of the countryside.

In the primitive society, all able-bodied people participated in labor. There was no specialization in mental labor. In the slave society, the situation was different. As a result of a large quantity of surplus products created by slave labor, it was possible for the slave owners to divorce themselves from production labor. At that time, the division between mental and physical labor was necessary and possible. This division between mental and physical labor was antagonistic right from the start. It was the privilege of the slave-owning class to enjoy cultural education. 'The class controlling the means of material production also controlled the means of mental production. Therefore, the thinking of those without means of mental production was generally under the influence of the ruling class." (7) The slave-owning class tried its best to spread the fallacy that "the mental workers rule others while the physical laborers are ruled by others." It used to its best advantage its politics, law, philosophy, and ideology as tools to rule the slaves and other laboring masses for the consolidation of the dictatorship of the slave owner.

The Rebellion of Slaves Hastened the Collapse of Slavery

Slavery was an inevitable stage in human history. Its appearance met the needs of existing productive forces. Under slavery, prisoners of war were no longer slaughtered enmasse. They were instead kept alive to work. This was helpful to the development of production. Because the slave owner possessed large amounts of means of production and labor, it was possible to organize production and cooperation on a large scale. With the use of metal tools, agriculture, animal husbandry, and handicraft industry developed rapidly. Agriculture became the most important component of the national economy. The horse, buffalo, sheep, chicken, dog and pig were domesticated. By means of cooperative efforts among a large number of handicraftsmen, a bronze ritual vessel [ssu-mu-ma o ta fang ting] measuring 110 centimeters in horizontal length, 77 centimeters in width, 137 centimeters in height, and weighing 1,400 market catties, was cast with fine floral designs. From it we can infer the high production skills and workmanship already reached at that time.

The production relations of the slave society promoted the development of productive forces to a certain extent. But these production relations embodied inherent contradictions to the further development of productive forces. These contradictions became more acute as productive forces developed. The broad masses of slaves could not bear the cruel exploitation and oppression of the slave owner any longer. They slowed their work, ran away in large numbers, and purposely wrecked production tools. On the one hand, the slave owners increased their oppression, leadingto massive early death of slaves. On the other hand, they substituted heavy tools not easily subject to abuse. But the development of productive forces was thus restricted. The restriction on the development of productive forces also resulted from the contempt toward physical labor generated by the system. Bankrupt small producers preferred to wander around than to engage in physical labor. These things all showed that the production relations of slavery were already ill-suited to the development of productive forces. Its extinction was as inevitable as its emergence.

At the end of the slave society, feudal production relations appeared. The ownership of land by the slave state was the basis of the production relations in the slave society. In the Yin-Chou period of China, state ownership of land was in the form of ching-t'ien [well fields]. All land within the confines of chin g-t'ien was called "communal land." These "communal lands" and the slaves were at the disposal of the biggest slave owners — the feudal princes, nobles, and state officials appointed by the Son of Heaven. With the development of productive forces, some slave owners tried their best to force the slaves to bring under cultivation large amounts of "private land" so as to exploit more surplus labor. With the expansion of "private land," the system of "communal land" was undermined. At this time, the landlord class emerged. They championed the "abolition of ching-t'ien and the demolition of raised paths between fields [used as boundaries]." Slaves gradually became serfs. The sprouts of feudal production relations flourished.

The basic classes of the slave society were the slave-owning class and the slaves. Outside of these two classes were the free peasants and handicraftsmen. Slaves were at the bottom of the social strata and were subject to the crudest exploitation and oppression by the slave owners. All through the whole period of slavery, there was violent class struggle between the slaves and the slave owners. The Spring and Autumn period of China saw the transition from slavery to feudalism. A slave leader named Chih led 9,000 people rampaging across the land and invading the feudal lords. Slave rebellions seriously challenged the rule of the slave-owning class. In various countries of the world, slave uprisings were the theme of many heroic epics. For example, in the Roman period, Spartacus led the biggest rebellion with 120,000 participants. This rebellion shook the whole Roman Empire to its foundation. Violent slave rebellions dealt severe blows to the political power of the slave owners and hastened the collapse of slavery. While slavery disintegrated, feudal production relations gradually matured. The newly emerging landlords representing feudal production relations used the power of the laboring people to overthrow the rule of the slave owners and established a government of landlords. Feudalism finally replaced slavery.

The replacement of slavery by feudalism was historically inevitable. In China, during the time of the great epoch-making social changes, Confucius, the reactionary proponent of the slave system, obstinately opposed any social reforms and regarded the changes in production relations as "great evils."

He resolutely opposed all the reform measures carried out by the new feudal lords, advocated the restoration of the old slave system, and hoped in vain to save the tottering social order. But it was all over. His efforts represented the futile struggle of a dying cause.

Feudalism Is Another Exploitative System Based on Class Conflicts

Feudal Landownership Is the Economic Substructure of the Feudal Society

The production relations of the feudal society were based on landownership by the landlord class and their almost complete control of serfs. The landlord owned most of the land. The peasants and serfs owned little or no land. They had to depend on farming the landlord's land for a living. This way, they were fettered by the feudal land system. They lost their personal freedom and were subject to the landlord's cruel exploitation and oppression.

The chief means by which the landlord exploited the peasants was through the collection of feudal rent from land rented to them. There were three kinds of feudal rents: labor rent, rent in kind, and money rent.

Labor rent was prevalent in the early period of the feudal society. Labor rent consisted of the peasants using their own tools and working on the landlord-operated land at specified times. The peasants could work on their land only after working for the landlord. Under this type of land rent, the relations between the exploiter and the exploited were quite clear-cut.

The produce from the land operated by the peasants belonged to them. They were thus interested in the labor performed on it. The produce from the labor performed by the peasants on the land operated by the landlord belonged wholly to the landlord. The peasants were naturally not enthusiastic about such labor. The landlord was well aware of this difference in attitude. To make the peasants work hard on the land operated by the landlord, the latter kept a number of foremen to enforce strict discipline. Therefore, under such a rent system, the relations between the oppressor and the oppressed, the ruling and ruled, were quite obvious. In the early period of feudalism, productive forces were quite weak. The landlord could not have expropriated the surplus labor of the peasants if he had not relied on direct coercion. This kind of feudal rent met with violent resistance from the peasants.

Later, under the impetus of the development of productive forces and out of a desire for greater exploitation and less visibility of their exploitative intent, the landlord adopted rent in kind in place of labor rent. Under rent in kind, the peasant no longer worked under the supervision of the landlord. He did not have to work on the land operated by the landlord. The peasant could control all his labor. But he had to turn in surplus produce in kind to the landlord at specified intervals. Compared with labor rent, rent in kind was instrumental in improving know-how and labor productivity to some extent. But rent in kind often represented 50 percent or even 70 to 80 percent of the peasants' harvests. To maintain a minimum level of subsistence, the peasants had to extend their working hours and raise their labor intensity. Even so, the peasants were unable to lead a life very far above extreme poverty.

Money rent appeared in late feudal society. Productive force were then much higher than before. The relations between money and commodities were widely developed. To satisfy his manifold needs for a luxurious and extravagant life, the landlord needed ever more money. Under such conditions, money rent appeared. Under money rent, the peasants sold their produce in the market in exchange for money to pay rent. Thus the peasants were not only exploited by the landlord, but also by merchant middlemen. When harvests were good, the merchant! depressed prices to squeeze every drop of sweat and blood from the peasants. As a result, the peasants' livelihood was even more pitiable, and they were frequently at the brink of bankruptcy.

In the feudal society, the broad masses of peasants were under the exploitation of feudal rent. They also had to pay heavy taxes to the feudal state and were subject to the exploitation of usurers. The landlord colluded with the bureaucrats and the army to plunder the peasants' land, steal their wealth, and force them to engage in involuntary unpaid labor. The broad masses of peasants were subject to all sorts of extraeconomic exploitation

Peasant Rebellions Reflected the Increasingly Acute Class Contradictions in the Feudal Society

The replacement of the slave society by the feudal society was a step forward in history. The feudal production relations were conducive to promoting productive forces in the early stage of feudal society. Agricultural production techniques were elevated, and tools improved. The applications of iron instruments to production were disseminated, both the variety and quantity of crops were increased, and handicraft industry was thriving. In the Warring States period of China, large-scale water conservancy projects, such as the Tu-chiang Dike in Szechuan Province, were constructed. Through additional construction and maintenance during various dynasties, Tu-chiang Dike still serves a very useful purpose at present. Salt baking, metallurgy, silk goods, spinning and weaving, porcelain and pottery, and embroidery were quite well developed in China's feudal society. The compass, gunpowder, paper, and block printing were invented very early.

However, production under feudal production relations was basically small-scale production on a household basis. This small-scale production was not conducive to the further development of productive forces. The broad masses of peasants under feudal production relations were especially subject to cruel exploitation and oppression with little possibility for developing production. The contradictions between feudal production relations and productive forces were reflected as class contradictions between the landlord and the peasant. This was the major contradiction in feudal society. The highest manifestation of this contradiction was armed rebellion by the broad masses of peasants to resist the rule of the landlord. These rebellions and struggles were characteristic of the whole feudal period. About 200 B.C., soon after Ch'in Shih-huang unified China and established the first feudal dictatorship, the first great peasant rebellion in China's history exploded — the rebellion led by Ch'en Sheng and Wu Kuang. After that, during the more than two thousand years before the Taiping Rebellion in the mid-nineteenth century, several hundred small and large peasant rebellions and peasant revolutionary wars were recorded. The size and number of peasant uprisings in Chinese history broke world records. "Only these peasant class struggles, peasant rebellions, and peasant wars were the real motive force of historical development. Because every major peasant rebellion and peasant war dealt blows to the contemporary feudal rule, they thus promoted the development of social productive forces to some extent." (8) However, renegades like Ch'en Po-ta attributed the development of social productive forces to the "concessions" made by the feudal ruling class. This runs counter to historical facts. In history, the landlords never madi concessions to peasant rebellions. They always resorted to bloodthirsty suppression, counterattacks, and trickery, but never to "concessions." Renegade Ch'en Po-ta's theory about "concessions" was purely an attempt to beautify the landlords.

The Development of a Commodity Economy and Primitive Accumulation Gave Birth to and Promoted Capitalist Production Relations

In the late feudal period, with the further development of a commodity economy, capitalist production relations arose.

Simple commodity production in the feudal society was based on private ownership and individual labor. The purpose of production was exchange. Small commodity producers had to sell their products in the market. But because every commodity producer had different production conditions, skills, and labor intensity, labor spent on each type of commodity varied. On the other hand, similar commodities were sold at the same price. This constituted a contradiction. With the development of this contradiction, a small number of small commodity producers with better conditions prospered. But the majority of small commodity producers with poorer production conditions were increasingly impoverished. Thus, the simple commodity producers were polarized.

In the feudal society, craft guilds were often formed to prevent competition among handicraftsmen in the same line or from handicraftsmen from other areas or lines. Members of the guilds had to obey guild regulations. In the handicraft guild, there were the master, journeyman, and apprentice. The relations between the master and the journeyman and apprentice were basically feudal with slight exploitation. These guilds limited the polarization among the small commodity producers. But with the development of a commodity economy, some comparatively prosperous masters were unwilling to obey the guild regulations. They indiscriminately increased the number of journeymen and apprentices, lengthened their labor time, improved production techniques, and gradually converted their journeymen and apprentices into hired hands. Other bankrupt masters, journeymen, and apprentices gradually joined the ranks of hired hands. On the basis of polarization, there gradually appeared the capitalist relations of employment.

In the process of polarization among the small commodity producers and the emergence of capitalist production relations, commercial capital played an important role. The merchant was originally the middleman in commodity exchange. Later he became a contract merchant who contracted to sell the products of the commodity producers. He later supplied raw materials and even tools to the small producers who were to produce products at specified times and of a certain quality, quantity, type, and specification. Thus, the small commodity producer was entirely controlled by the merchant and became a hired hand. And the merchant himself became an industrial capitalist.

In the countryside, during the period of late feudal society, because of the development of a commodity economy, the landlord class gradually converted to money rents. This daily increased the peasants 1 dependence on markets and hastened their polarization. The majority of peasants went bankrupt and degenerated into hired farm hands. A few elevated themselves to become rich peasants and later agricultural capitalists.

Thus, capitalist production relations gradually established themselves in feudal society. In China's late feudal society, with the development of a commodity economy, the seeds of capitalist production relations were about to sprout. Without the influence of foreign capitalism, China was gradually to develop into a capitalist society.

The establishment of capitalist production relations in feudal society was closely related to the development of productive forces. In the beginning, the small workshops of the handicraftsmen became large capitalist workshops. In these workshops, hand labor was still the rule. But with many workers working together under unified capitalist command, simple cooperation was possible, forming a new productive force. Later, capitalist simple cooperation developed into capitalist factory handicraft industry. The characteristic of the factory handicraft industry was division of labor among workers producing the same commodity with each specializing in one process. It simplified labor processes and improved labor productivity by intensifying labor input. It also created the conditions for the substitution of machine operation for hand operation.

The development of capitalist production relations depended on two basic conditions: First, there had to be a large body of proletariat who could freely sell their labor. Second, there had to be a prior accumulation of a large amount of pecuniary wealth To facilitate the development of capitalist production relations, the bourgeoisie used violence to create these two conditions. Therefore, in the development of capitalism, there was a process of primitive accumulation.

An important method of primitive accumulation was exploitation of the peasant. England, where capitalist production relations first developed, was a typical example. During the more than three hundred years from the 1470s until the early nineteenth century, the English ruling class launched the "enclosure" movement by forcibly taking land from the peasants. The modem industry of England started from wool textiles. The wool textile industry required a large amount of wool, thus forcing up its price. The big landlords and farm operators enclosed land wherever they could to raise sheep to cash in on the fortune. They forcibly evicted peasants from their land, demolished and burned down their houses, and expropriated large amounts of means of production and means of livelihood. The enclosure movement forced a large number of peasants to leave their native places and wander far afield begging for their livelihood. Following this, the English ruling class promulgated various bloodstained legislation to forbid the peasants from drifting and force them to accept hired employment under harsh conditions.

The plundering of pecuniary wealth was another important method of primitive accumulation. The European bourgeoisie resorted to armed invasions of Asia, Africa, America, and Australia to establish the colonial system. They launched commercial warfare and plundered the colonies' material resources and pecuniary wealth in order to amass capital for the establishment of large-scale capitalist production.

Therefore, the process of primitive accumulation was the process of forcing the separation of the direct producers from their means of production and concentrating pecuniary wealth in the hands of the capitalists as capital. Marx penetratingly pointed out, "This history of expropriation (of the direct producers by the bourgeoisie) was written with blood and fire into the human chronology." (9) The process of primitive accumulation vividly demonstrated that the capitalists did not "start from scratch," but depended entirely on plundering. "Capital comes dripping from head to foot, from every pore, with blood and dirt." (10)

Bourgeois Revolution Declared the Collapse of Feudalism

The birth and development of capitalist production relations in feudal society was severely restricted by feudal production relations and their superstructure. They were prevented from assuming a dominating role in feudal society because the feudal ruling class would never willingly retire from the historical stage. They inevitably used the state machinery in their control to protect the outdated feudal system. The bourgeoisie and the intellectuals representing capitalist production relations publicized capitalist production relations as "manifestations 01 eternity and rationality" and "an eternal law of Nature." They championed so-called "freedom, equality, and universal love" and denounced feudalism in their efforts to prepare public opinion for the bourgeois revolution to overthrow feudalism. In the bourgeois revolution, the major class forces were the peasant! the proletariat, and the bourgeoisie. The peasants were the major force, but not the representatives of the new productive forces. The proletariat had not formed its independent political force, so the bourgeoisie assumed the leadership of the bourgeois revolution.

In old China, because it was a semi feudal and semicolonial society, the bourgeoisie was divided into two parts. One was the bureaucratic bourgeoisie. It depended on imperialism. Along with the landlords, its members represented the most backward and most reactionary production relations. They were the targets of the Chinese bourgeois democratic revolution. The second part was the national bourgeoisie. It was subject to the oppression and restriction of imperialism and feudalism on the one hand but was also closely related to them on the other. This determined that the national bourgeoisie was a force on the side of democratic revolution under some conditions. But it was also weak and unstable. Therefore, "it was determined historically that the task of anti-imperialist and antifeudal bourgeois democratic revolution could not be completed by bourgeois leadership, but only by proletarian leadership." (11),

Although the bourgeois revolution was a revolution in which one form of exploitation replaced another, this revolution also had its reversals. In the course of the revolution, there were acute class struggles involving attempted restorations by the feudal class and opposition to restorations by the bourgeoisie. England started its bourgeois revolution in 1640. Not until after two internal wars was Charles I, a representative of the Stuarts, executed. In 1660, Charles n, another representative of the Stuarts, again attempted restoration. In 1688, the English bourgeoisie invited the Prince of Orange (William HI) from Holland to overthrow the Stuart House. Only then was the bourgeois dictatorship stabilized. In France, in the eighty-six years from 1789 when the bourgeois revolution exploded until 1875 when the Third Republic was formed, advances were mixed with retreats, republics with monarchies, revolutionary terror with anti revolutionary terror, internal with external wars, conquests of with conquests by foreign countries, without a moment of peace and stability. Even so, because the feudal system was rotten, it still could not escape its extinction no matter how hard it tried to struggle. The replacement of feudalism by capitalism was inevitable.

Major Study References

Marx and Engels, Communist Manifesto.

Engels, The Origin of the Family, Private Prop e rty and the State.

Chairman Mao, "The Analysis of Chinese Social Classes." Chairman Mao, "The Chinese Revolution and the Chinese Communist Party," Chapter 1.

Revie w Problems

1. How did private ownership, classes, and the state arise?
2. How did the contradictions between production relations and productive forces in the slave society and the feudal society manifest themselves in class struggle?
3. What were the major conditions for the birth and development of capitalist production relations?

Notes

1) Engels, "The Role of Labor in the Transformation of Apes into Man," C omplete Works of Marx and Engels, Vol. 3, Jen‑ min ch'u‑pan‑she, 1972, p. 508.
2) Engels, Anti‑Duhring, Selected Works of Marx and Engels, Jen‑min ch'u‑pan‑she, 1972, p. 154.
3) "On Practice," Selected Works of Mao Tse‑tung, Vol. 1 Jen‑min ch'u‑pan‑she, 1968, p. 260.
4) "The Chinese Revolution and the Chinese Communist Part Sele cted Works of Mao Tse‑tung, Vol. 2, Jen‑min ch'u‑pan‑sh 1968, p.585.
5) Communist Manifesto, Selected Works of Marx and Engels, Vol. 1, Jen‑min ch'u‑pan‑she, 1972, p. 250.
6) "The Chinese Revolution and the Chinese Communist Part Selected Works of Mao Tse‑tung, Vol. 2, Jen‑min ch'u‑pan‑sh T%¥, p.585.

7) The German Ideology, Selected Works of Marx and Engels, Vol. 1, Jen-min ch'u-pan-she, 1972, p. 52.

8) "The Chinese Revolution and the Chinese Communist Party," Selected Works of Mao Tse-tung, Vol. 2, Jen-min ch'u-pan-sh 1968, p. 588.

9) Marx, Capital, Vol. 1, Complete Works of Marx and Engels, Vol. 23, p. 783.

10)   Ibid., p. 829.

11)   "The Task of the Chinese Communist Party in the Anti-Japanese Period," Selected Works of Mao Tse-tung, Vol. 1, Jen-min ch'u-pan-she, 1968, p. 241.

3, The Analysis of Capitalist Society Must Start from Commodities

Commodities, Money, and the Law of Value

Chairman Mao points out: Marx "started from the simplest capitalist factor — commodities — to analyze closely the economic structure of the capitalist society." (1) Why did Marx start from commodities in his analysis of capitalist economy? This is because every product in the capitalist society is a commodity. Not only are means of production and consumer goods commodities, even human labor is a commodity. Here, social wealth is reflected as a large amount of accumulated commodities. Commodities become the cell structures of the capitalist economy. In commodities are embodied all the contradictions of capitalism. Therefore, the study of capitalism must start from an analysis of commodities.

The Commodity Relation Embodies the Seeds of All Capitalist Contradictions

Commodities Consist of Two Components: A Use Value and an Exchange Value

Commodities, the product of labor, are for sale and exchange. They went through a historical process of birth and development. In the primitive society, people labored together. The products obtained were all consumed by the members of the primitive commune. Under these conditions, there was no exchange or production of commodities. The exchange and production of commodities developed gradually in the slave and feudal society. Their development reached a peak in the capitalist world.

What are the basic characteristics of commodities which are the cells of the capitalist economy?

Since commodities are labor products for exchange, they must first of all be useful to people. For example, rice can fill our stomachs, clothes can keep us warm, iron and steel can be made into machines, and tractors can plow. This usefulness of a commodity is called use value. Obviously, if something is not useful, nobody needs it. It cannot, therefore, qualify as a commodity.

Use value is a necessary condition of a commodity but not the only condition. Not all useful things are commodities. For example, air and sunshine are basic necessities for our survival, but they are not labor products. They are free goods and therefore not commodities. Further, though food grains and vegetables are labor products, if they are produced for one's own consumption, they are not commodities. Again, though food grains turned in by the peasant to the landlord as rent are not for the peasant's own consumption, they are not paid for by the landlord and cannot, therefore, be regarded as commodities.

Labor products can become commodities only if they are transferred to other people through exchange. Therefore, in addition to use value, commodities must also be exchangeable for other products. This characteristic of commodities is called exchange value.

Exchange value is first expressed as a numerical proportion between one use value and another use value. For example, one chang of cloth is exchanged for two tou of rice. The two tou of rice is the value in exchange for one chan g of cloth.

The numerical exchange proportion between two commodities varies according to time and place. But at a given time and place, this proportion is, on the whole, uniform. What determines this exchange proportion? Obviously, if various commodities can, in the course of exchange, establish among them numerical proportions, they must have something in common. This common property cannot be their use values. From the viewpoint of their use values, every commodity is different in nature. For example, cloth can be made into clothes, and rice can fill our stomachs. These are two entirely different use values and cannot be compared. The common property among the commodities must be found in their exchange value. And when the use value of both commodities, whether cloth or rice, is ignored, the only characteristic left is that they are both labor products. Labor has been expended for their production. This embodied labor constitutes value. Values are comparable, and therefore commodities can be compared in quantity. The fact that one chang of cloth can be exchanged for two tou of rice implies that their production requires an equal quantity of labor. Consequently, they are equal in value. Exchange value is therefore determined by value. Exchange value is an expression of value. Value itself is the basis of exchange value.

Use value and value are the two characteristics of commodities. They constitute the two factors of commodities. Use value is the material support for value. If one commodity has no use value, no matter how much labor has been expended on it, no value can be formed. And it cannot be a commodity in exchange for other labor products. At the same time, only use value created by labor can become the use value of commodities. Even if something is absolutely essential for our survival, such as air and sunshine, it cannot become a commodity unless labor has been expended on it.

The Duality of Commodities Is Determined by the Duality of Labor Used in Commodity Production

Where does the duality of commodities come from? When we go to the source, we discover that labor used for commodity production has a dual nature: it consists of concrete labor on the one hand and abstract labor on the other.

To produce various use values, people have to engage in various purposeful production activities. For example, carpenters make tables, and peasants raise crops. They all have their own tools, their objects, and their methods. The labor of a peasant consists of using various farm tools to plow, rake, plant, and harvest, finally producing food crops. This labor expended in different concrete forms is called concrete labor. Concrete labor creates use value. There are many different use values for commodities. There are also many different forms of concrete labor in commodity production. Concrete labor in various trades and occupations is different, a manifestation of a complex division of labor.

Various concrete labor is different in nature and cannot be compared. But in the market, various labor products can be compared. This shows that labor expended on commodity production not only has an aspect of difference, but also an aspect of similarity.

What is this similarity? It lies in the fact that although labor is different in its concrete forms for the production of various commodities, it is basically an expenditure of physical and mental human labor. This homogeneous labor abstracted from its concrete characteristics is called abstract labor. The value of commodities is created by abstract labor. Earlier, we said labor embodied in commodities constitutes value. Now, after analyzing the duality of labor, we can be more specific about the meaning of value. Value is the abstract labor embodied in commodities.

Concrete labor and abstract labor are not two different types of labor. They are merely two aspects of the same labor. People must engage in various forms of concrete labor in the production of various use values for the satisfaction of various needs. Concrete labor expresses the relation between man and Nature. On the other hand, abstract labor provides a unified measure to compare the labor expended on the production of various commodities. Therefore, abstract labor expresses the social relation in which labor is exchanged among people under the condition of commodity production.

The Value of Commodities Is Determined by the Socially Necessary Labor

The value of commodities is created by labor. Its level is determined by the labor expended on the production of commodities. And the volume of labor is measured by labor time. The longer the labor time needed for the production of a commodity, the larger the volume of labor and the higher the value.

Does this mean that the lazier and more unskilled a man is, the more valuable the commodity he produces would be? Definitely not.

The production of a given commodity requires different labor time from different commodity producers for obvious reasons. Some are more skilled than others. And some use better tools and equipment than others. The time required by those who are more skilled and use better tools and equipment is naturally shorter than the time required by those less skilled and using crude tools and equipment. Then, which labor time should be used to determine the value of commodities?

The labor time expended by various commodity producers on commodity production is called individual labor time. For example, some carpenters spend thirty hours to make a table, some twenty-five hours, and others twenty hours. These are all individual labor times. The value of commodities is not determined by the individual labor time, but by the socially necessary labor. "Socially necessary labor is such labor time as is required for producing a use value under existing normal conditions of production and with the average amount of skill and intensity prevalent at the time." (2) If under normal production conditions and with the average amount of skill and intensity the required time to make a table is twenty-five hours, then twenty-five hours are the socially necessary labor for making tables. Twenty-five hours' labor is the socially necessary labor determining the value of a table.

When we talk about labor determining value, we must distinguish between not only individual labor and socially necessary labor, but also between simple labor and complex labor. Simple labor is labor that can be performed by a normal, healthy person without going through special training. Complex labor is labor performed by a skilled worker who has undergone certain special training. Therefore, in a given period of time, the value created by simple labor is less than that created by complex labor. Complex labor is multiple simple labor. The conversion between complex and simple labor is spontaneously carried out in the exchange process.

The Contradiction between Private Labor and Social Labor Is the Basic Contradiction of Commodity Production

We have analyzed above the duality of commodities, the duality of labor in commodity production, and the value of commodities. With this basic understanding, we can further analyze the contradictions of commodity production.

Commodities are used as exchange for labor products. Commodity producers produce commodities not for their own needs, but for sale in exchange for the commodities they need. For example, the blacksmith does not make hoes because he needs them. What he is concerned about is selling the hoes to realize their value for the exchange of the rice and cloth he needs. Whether his commodities can be sold or not is of vital concern to the commodity producer.

Commodities are a unifier between the opposites of use value and value. Concrete labor and abstract labor in commodity production are also opposites in unity. They are unified in a commodity, but they are also opposites. If the commodity can be sold, their internal contradictions are resolved. When a hoe reaches the hands of a peasant who needs it, concrete labor is converted into abstract labor, and the blacksmith obtains the value of his hoe. The use value and the value of the hoe are also unified. But if the commodity cannot be sold, the contradiction between use value and value and the contradiction between concrete labor and abstract labor are immediately revealed. Although the hoe obviously possesses use value, if it cannot be sold, its value cannot be realized, and the hoe is no better than a heap of scrap. In this case, the concrete labor of the blacksmith, which also obviously represents the expenditure of physical and mental labor, cannot be converted into abstract labor. In other words, his labor is not recognized by society and is as good as wasted. Under these conditions, the blacksmith has no means to purchase pig iron and charcoal with which to engage in more production. He certainly has no means to buy fuel, rice, oil, and salt to support himself. The contradictions between use value and value and between concrete and abstract labor bear directly upon the production and livelihood of the commodity producer.

How do these contradictions in commodity production arise? Where are their origins? There is one basic contradiction in commodity production under private ownership. This is the contradiction between private and social labor. Since commodities are labor products used for exchange and since the use value created by the producer is not for the satisfaction of his own needs but to satisfy social needs, the labor of the commodity producer is social in nature. It is a part of total social labor. But under the condition of private ownership, what and how much to produce and the size of his income are the private affairs of the producer. Therefore, the labor of the commodity producer also possesses the nature of private labor. This contradiction between private and social labor is the source of all contradictions of commodity production under private ownership. When the commodities produced by the private producer are sold in the market, it shows that his private labor is recognized by society and constitutes a part of the social labor. If the commodities cannot be sold, the private labor of the commodity producer is not recognized by society and cannot be converted into social labor. The concrete labor of the commodity producer cannot be converted into abstract labor. The value of commodities cannot, therefore, be realized.

Marx's Labor Theory of Value Is the Basis of the Theory of Surplus Value

Through the analysis of the duality of labor, Marx firmly created the labor theory of value. This theory scientifically demonstrates that concrete labor creates the use value of commodities, while abstract labor creates the value of commodities and labor is the sole source of value. Marx's labor theory of value is the basis of Marx's theory of surplus value and is an important constituent part of Marxist political economy.

Before the proletariat received the guidance of Marxist theory, they did not realize the source of their sufferings and coul< not identify the objects of their struggle. Some mistakenly thought that their sufferings were caused by machines and once resorted to destroying machines as a method of struggle. Marx summarized the long experience of the proletarian struggle and created the theory of surplus value to expose the secret of capitalist exploitation. This made the proletariat realize their historical mission and the fact that only through violent revolution and the replacement of capitalism by socialism could they be liberated. Marx's theory of surplus value is based on the labor theory of value. Without the labor theory of value, the theory of surplus value could not have been established.

Because Marx's labor theory of value provided theoretical guidance to proletarian revolutionary struggles, bourgeois economists tried their best to establish all sorts of anti‑ scientific theories of value in a vain attempt to separate the relations between value and labor, to oppose Marx's labor theory of value, and to conceal capitalist exploitation.

Among the vulgar economists, a production-costs theory of value was once much in vogue. This theory says that the value of a commodity is determined by the costs of production (the value of the means of production and labor wages) expended on its production. If the value of a commodity is in fact determined by the costs of production, then the capitalist would only get back the costs of production expended when the commodity is sold. How can he ever get rich this way? Where is the exploitation of the worker? Therefore, those vulgar economists who proposed that value was determined by the cost of production necessarily explained profit as a form of higher wage, a reward for abstinence, an award for risk. This fully exposed their ugly role as apologists for the bourgeoisie.

Among the bourgeois vulgar economists, another utility theory of value was also once in vogue. According to this theory, the value of a commodity is determined by the amount of utility it possesses. What then is "utility"? This is, in fact, the use value of a commodity. We said earlier that various commodities had different use values which were not comparable. It is simply not logical to say that the value of a commodity is determined by its use value. The utility theorists of value could not intelligently explain why such things as air and sunshine, which are essential for human survival, did not possess any value and could not be sold as commodities.

Another popular theory among the bourgeois vulgar economists was a supply-demand theory of value. This theory denied that there was any objective, intrinsic value in a commodity and thought that the value of commodities was determined by the supply and demand conditions in the market. When the supply of a certain commodity exceeded its demand, its exchange value for other commodities was lower, and its value was lower. But when the demand for a commodity exceeded its supply, its exchange value for other commodities was higher, and its value was higher. This theory was obviously fallacious. The supply-demand theorists of value simply cannot explain what determines the value of a commodity when supply is equal to demand; neither can they explain why, in the changing relations between supply and demand for various commodities, some commodities are consistently more expensive than others.

Although the bourgeois economists tried their best to negate the labor theory of value, truth can never be negated. Marxist labor theory of value has been proven to be the only correct theory in its struggle against various pseudoscientific theories of the bourgeoisie.

Money Is a Natural Product of the Development of Commodity Exchange

Money Is a Special Commodity Serving as a Universal Equivalent

Money is associated with commodities because in daily life the value of commodities is expressed in terms of money. And commodities are bought with money. However, the value of commodities was not expressed in terms of money from the start. Money is a product of the development of commodity production and exchange.

Commodity exchange started out as direct barter among com modities. In the beginning, the nomad tribes and agricultural tribes exchanged their surplus products. For example, sheep were exchanged for rice. At that time, the exchange of commodities was on an occasional basis and occurred mainly among clan communes. In the course of exchange, the value of a commodity was accidentally expressed in terms of another commodity. For example, two sheep equal one bag of rice. The value of a sheep could not be evaluated in terms of itself. But when sheep were exchanged for rice, the value of a sheep was expressed in terms of rice. In the above equation, commodities such as rice assumed the special role of an "equivalent." They acted like a mirror and in them the value of another commodity could be reflected.

With the development of productive forces and social division of labor, commodity exchange daily developed. Both the volume and the variety of commodities being exchanged increased. In the course of exchange, one commodity could be traded for many other commodities. Its value could be expressed in many other commodities. At the same time, with the development of commodity exchange, the disadvantages of direct barter among commodities were increasingly evident. Direct barters could be concluded only when both sides happened to need what the other side had to offer. For example, suppose that the owner of sheep wanted to exchange them for food grains, but the owner of food grains needed a hoe instead of sheep and the owner of hoes wanted cloth instead of sheep or food grains. If the owner of cloth happened to want sheep, then, the seller of sheep could obtain food grains by first exchanging sheep for cloth, then cloth for hoes, and finally hoes for food grains. The expected purpose of exchange was realized only after much trouble. If the owner of cloth did not need sheep, then no matter how much trouble he went through, he still could not get what he wanted. Therefore, when commodity production increasingly developed, direct barters proved to be extremely difficult.

In the course of commodity exchange, people gradually realized that if they first exchanged what they had for some commodity (like sheep) which was generally needed and used it to exchange for what they needed, then the purpose of exchange could be realized in only two transactions. Therefore, in the long developmental process of commodity exchange, commodities such as sheep would be separated from other commodities and perform a role not possible for other commodities. Then, the values of all commodities were all expressed in terms of sheep. And sheep assumed the role of a "universal equivalent" in commodity exchange.

In the long process of the development of commodity exchange, nations used different mediums of exchange, including sheep, shells, cloth, and metals. Finally, they decided to use precious metals such as gold and silver as money. Because the precious metals are small in quantity but great in value, easy to carry, readily divisible, and not perishable, they are suitable for a medium of exchange. Hence, gold and silver are generally accepted as money. Note, however, that money is not an innate property of gold and silver; it is acquired. Gold and silver became money under certain historical production relations.

From the origin of money, one can understand the nature of money. Money is a special commodity separated from other commodities and serving as a medium of exchange.

The Five Functions of Money Evolved Step by Step

The property of money is manifested in its functions. Money possesses five functions which are evolved in the process of commodity exchange. These functions are to serve as (1) a unit of value, (2) a medium of exchange, (3) a standard of payments, (4) a store of value, and (5) a universal currency. Of these, the basic functions are as a unit of value and as a medium of exchange. But they have all evolved with the emergence of money

The first function of money is as a unit of value. Just as a ruler is used to measure the length of things, money is used to measure the value of commodities. Money functioning as a measure of value can be conceptual money. This is to say, when people use money to evaluate the value of commodities, they need not have money in their hands. For example, a table is worth ten yuan. But there is no need to put ten yuan on the table. When the values of commodities are expressed in terms of money, they are the prices of the commodities. Prices are the expression of values in money terms. The prices of commodities are determined by two factors. One is the value of the commodities themselves, and the other is the value of money (gold, silver). The prices of commodities are directly proportional to the value of the commodities themselves and inversely proportional to the value of money. For example, a buffalo is worth five hundred hours of social labor and one ounce of gold is worth five hundred hours of social labor. Then, the price of a buffalo is one ounce of gold. If the labor productivity of gold miners is doubled and one ounce of gold is now worth only two hundred and fifty hours of social labor, then, even though the value of a buffalo has not changed a bit, the price of a buffalo has doubled.

The second function of money is as a medium of exchange, namely, it serves as a medium of commodity circulation. Commodity circulation is commodity exchange by means of money. Before the appearance of money, commodities were bartered directly. In terms of a formula, it is expressed as commodity equals commodity. After the appearance of money, all commodities were exchanged in terms of money. In terms of a formula, it is expressed as commodity equals money equals commodity. This role of money as a medium in commodity circulation is the function of money as a medium of exchange.

The money used as a medium of exchange was originally gold and silver pieces of different sizes and weights. This was later replaced by coins. Coins were merely minted metal pieces of uniform shape, purity, and weight certified by the state. The coins of various countries were all different. In China's late Shang dynasty, coins began to be minted with copper. The oldest coins were made of copper and shaped like farm tools. They were known as p u ch'ie n. In the Chou dynasty, in addition to pu ch'ien, there were t ao ch'ie n and yuan c h'ien. Yin yuan [silver dollars] were first minted in the Kuang-hsii period of the Ch'ing dynasty. Each yin yuan consisted of 0.72 ounces of silver.

In the course of circulation, coins were worn out and part of their value was lost. But even then coins were still accepted at their full value. This was because the function of money as a medium of exchange was performed in one instant. People exchanged their commodities for money merely in order to use it to buy the commodities they needed. The primary concern of the commodity owners was whether the money could be used as a medium of exchange and not whether the money had its full worth. For this reason, not only could worn metal money be used as a medium of exchange, but even pure value symbols in the form of paper notes could take its place.

Since paper money in place of metal money serves as a medium of exchange in commodity circulation, the amount of paper money issued is limited to the amount of metal money needed for commodity circulation. Marx pointed out: "The amount of paper money issued, which is a token or symbol of real money, always equals the value of the gold (or silver) needed for commodity circulation." (3) If the paper money issued equals the amount of metal money needed for commodity circulation, then the paper money shall possess the same purchasing power as the metal money. If the amount of paper money issued exceeds the amount of metal money needed for commodity circulation, then the value of the total paper money still equals the metal money needed for commodity circulation, but the unit value of the paper money shall fall in terms of the metal money. Hence, the value of the paper money depreciates, and commodity prices appreciate. For example, if, in a given period, the amount of metal money needed for circulation were 100 million yuan but the amount of paper money were 200 million yuan, then the value of paper money would be halved. The purchasing power of 1 yuan of paper money would be equivalent only to 0.5 yuan of metal money.

This depreciation of paper money resulting from the issue of paper money in excess of the amount of metal money needed for circulation is called inflation. In capitalist society, inflation is an important means by which the bourgeois state plunders its people. The result of inflation is the depreciation of paper money and rising prices. On the other hand, the increases in the money wages of the workers lag far behind the increases in prices, resulting in decreases of their real wages and their standard of living. At the same time, the exploitative income of the bourgeoisie increases rapidly. In old China, the issue of legal tender reached astronomical figures, leading to galloping inflation and quantum jumps in prices. Some people once calculated that the purchasing power of 100 yuan of legal tender in 1937 was two buffaloes. In 1938, it was one buffalo. In 1941, it was one pig. In 1947, it was one-third of a box of matches. In 1948, it could not even buy one-third of a matchstick.

The third function of money is as a means of hoarding. The development of the money relation of commodities increasingly made money into a symbol of social wealth. When the natural economy played a dominant role, the accumulation of wealth assumed the form of food grains, cloth, and silk goods. After the money relation of commodities was developed, because money could be used to purchase any commodity, the accumulation of wealth increasingly adopted the form of hoarding money (gold and silver). This money which was temporarily.retired from commodity circulation and hoarded by its owner became hoarded money. It served the function as a means of hoarding.

The fourth function of money is as a means of payment. With the development of commodity production and exchange, transactions on credit increasingly developed. When a debt was due, payment had to be made in money. But at that time, commodity exchange had already been completed. Here, money no longer served as a medium of exchange, but rather as a means of payment. As a means of payment, money was first used among commodity producers to settle debts. Later, its use went beyond the sphere of commodity circulation. This function was also instrumental in the payment of rent, interest, and taxes.

The fifth function of money is as a world currency. With commodity exchange proceeding beyond a nation-state, international trade developed, and a new function of money was created. This was the function of a world currency. Only gold and silver could serve as world currency.

In the world market, gold first served as a means of payment to settle international accounts. This was the major function of a world currency. Next, in the world market, gold was also used as a means of payment to buy various commodities. Finally, gold was transferred from one country to another as a symbol of social wealth. For example, the payment of war indemnities, capital export, and other transfers of gold and silver from one country to another served this function.

The above five functions of money are organically related and are different expressions of the nature of money. They are the expressions of the different roles assumed by a universal equivalent in the development of commodity circulation.

The Law of Value Is the Economic Law of Commodity Production

The Objective Requirement of the Law of Value Is Equivalence in Exchange

The law of value is the economic law of commodity production and exchange. The basic content of this law is this: The value of a commodity is determined by the socially necessary labor. Commodities must be exchanged according to their values. That is, there must be equivalence in exchange. Wherever and whenever the conditions of a commodity economy exist, the law of value has a role to play. Marx said, "In the anarchic and constantly changing trade relations of private labor products, the socially necessary labor time for their production forcibly clears its own path as a regulatory law of nature, just as the law of gravity forcibly clears its own path when a house falls on a person's head." (4) In other words, in commodity exchange, although because of the influence of the supply-demand relation the proportions in which commodities are exchanged } may change continuously so that the socially necessary labor (the value) embodied in two commodities being exchanged may not be exactly equal, in the long run, commodity exchange necessarily involves equivalence in exchange. The values being exchanged must be identical.

Why is the objective tendency of commodity exchange toward equivalence in exchange? This is because commodity produced are all concerned about how much of others' commodities their own commodities can be exchanged for. Due to the influence of | the supply-demand relations, the proportions in which commodities are exchanged constantly change. People increase production of commodities which are more profitable and decrease in production of commodities that are less profitable. As a result, the supply of the former commodities exceeds the demand for them, and their exchange values decrease. The supply of 1 the latter commodities falls below the demand for them, and ! their exchange values increase. This constant change in the J proportions at which commodities are exchanged demonstrates! that equivalence in exchange is an objective law which does not] change according to people's will. With the appearance of money, all commodity exchanges de-' pend on money as a medium. Values are expressed as prices. The law of value requires equivalence in exchange. In other words, it requires the equivalence between prices and values.

Needless to say, the equivalence between prices and values must be understood as a long-term tendency. In fact, in a commodity economy based on private ownership in which production is uncoordinated, there are constant dislocations in the supply of and demand for commodities in the market, leading to constant fluctuations of prices. Although changes in the supply- demand relations lead to fluctuations in prices, the fluctuations are always centered around the equilibrium values. Therefore, nonequivalence between prices and values due to the influence of the supply-demand relations does not imply the negation of the law of value, but rather a necessary form through which the law of value operates.

The Three Functions of the Law of Value Which Arise in the Course of Market Competition

The law of value performs three functions in commodity production based on private ownership. These functions are realized through the spontaneous force of market competition.

First, the law of value is a regulator of production. It spontaneously regulates the distribution of social labor and the means of production among various production sectors. Commodity production based on private ownership is conducted under the condition of competition and anarchy. Nobody has direct information on what or how much society needs. But some order, allocations, and arrangements are necessary for the continuation of social production. These allocations and arrangements are regulated by the law of value and realized through the spontaneous influence of market price fluctuations. If the supply of a certain commodity does not meet the demand for it, its price will rise above its value, and the production of this commodity becomes especially profitable. The production of this commodity will thereby be increased. If the reverse is true, its price will fall below its value, and its production will be decreased. It is in this way that the law of value directs the activities of commodity producers and regulates the distribution of labor and the means of production among various production sectors.

Although the regulation of social production by the law of value imposes certain order in the commodity economy based on private ownership, this order is achieved under the condition of anarchy. It is constantly destroyed by blind competition, and a new order is again spontaneously formed. The establishment of this kind of order is achieved through an immense waste of social labor. Just as Marx said, "This orderless motion is its order." (5)

Second, the law of value stimulates the improvement of production techniques and labor productivity. Labor productivity is measured by the amount of products produced in one unit of time. Expressed as a formula: labor productivity equals amount of products divided by labor time. The level of labor productivity is determined by many factors. The most important ones are the skill of labor, the state of technology and its application to production, and the extent of division of labor and cooperation. According to the objective requirement of the law of value, commodities are sold according to the values determined by the socially necessary labor. Therefore, whoever is more skilled, more efficient, and uses less than the socially necessary labor time will get more profit. This stimulates the commodity producer to pay attention to improving his production techniques and labor productivity. But under private ownership, the improvement of production techniques by the commodity producer is for the sake of higher profits. Those who possess new techniques will naturally keep them secret. Under * these conditions, the development of social productive forces is hindered.

Third, the law of value promotes polarization among commodity producers. This is because the production conditions of various commodity producers are all different. The individual labor time used to produce a certain commodity varies widely. But the law of value requires that commodities are sold according to the value determined by the socially necessary labor. Thus, those commodity producers with better production facilities and with individual labor time less than the socially necessary labor time will make a higher profit and develop faster. On the other hand, those commodity producers with poorer production facilities and with individual labor time higher than the socially necessary labor time will not survive the competition. Thus, the polarization among commodity producers is inevitable.

Expose the Mystery of Commodity Fetishism

Fetishism originally referred to religions in which people worshiped things believed to possess certain mystical power. When the level of social productive forces was low and the control people exercised over Nature was weak, they made natural forces mysterious. They thought natural forces like thunder, lightning, water, and fire were controlled by certain gods and therefore worshiped them. This also happened in the commodity economy under private ownership. Although commodities are made by people's hands, they were worshiped as gods and believed to hold people's destiny. Marx called this phenomenon commodity fetishism.

How did commodity fetishism come about?

Under private ownership commodity production, the relations among men were manifested in commodity relations. Commodities were treated as if they were something above men, their master. The destiny of the commodity producer was entirely associated with the destiny of commodities. His destiny was entirely determined by whether and how well his commodities could be sold. If his commodities could be sold at profitable prices, the commodity producer would be well off. But if they could not be sold or could only be sold at very low prices, he would be poor. The commodity producer had no way of knowing beforehand whether there was a demand for his commodities or whether the commodities could be sold at good prices. The prices of commodities were not determined by the individual producers, but rather by the spontaneous forces of the operation of the law of value in the market. It was this condition that led the commodity producer to feel that his destiny was beyond his own control and was decided by the fate of his commodities in the market.

After the appearance of money as a universal equivalent which could be freely exchanged for all commodities, there arose an illusion that money itself had a special magical power that could affect people's destiny. Therefore, commodity fetishism inevitably developed into money fetishism.

Marx was the first one to reveal the mystery of commodity fetishism. Marx's theory on the relations between commodities and money permitted the revelation of the relations among people, while bourgeois economists could see only the relations among things and the social relations among them concealed by things. Marx's theory irrefutably demonstrated that the relation between commodities and money will not hold eternally, but will be a passing historical phenomenon. Therefore, the capitalist economic system with commodities as its cells is not eternal. Things that were created under certain historical conditions will disappear when the historical conditions change. This is an objective law that cannot be changed according to people's will.

Major Study References

Marx, Capital, Vol. 1, Chapters 1, 3.

Engels, Anti-Duhring, Part 2, Chapter 5.

Lenin, Karl Marx, ("Marx's Economic Theories").

Review Problems

1. Why do we say that commodity relations embody all the seeds of capitalist contradictions?
2. What are the major content and meanings of Marx's labor theory of value?
3. What are the roles played by the law of value in a commodity economy based on private ownership?

Notes

1) "The Rectification of the Party's Style of Work," Selected Works of Mao Tse-tun g, Vol. 3, Jen-min ch'u-pan-she, 1968,
2) Marx, Capital, Vol. 1, Complete Works of Marx and Engels, Vol. 23, p. 52.
3) Tbid., p. 147.
4) Ibid., p. 92.
5) Marx, Wage Labor and Capital, Selected Works of Marx and Engels, Vol. 1, Jen-min ch'u-pan-she, 1972, p. 360.

4. How the Capitalists Exploit and Oppress the Workers

Capital and Surplus Value

Capitalist production is commodity production aimed at reap ing surplus value. To understand the nature of capitalist production, we must study Marx's theory of capital and surplus value. Only by equipping ourselves with this theory can we understand the exploitative relation of capitalism, realize the inevitable extinction of capitalism and the inevitable triumph of socialism, appreciate the historical mission of the proletariat, and become conscious revolutionary soldiers of the proletariat.

The Secret of the Exploitation of the Workers by the Capitalists

The Conversion of Labor Power into Commodities Is the Precondition for the Production Surplus Value

Every old worker from the old society has a family history full of hardship and suffering. In the old society, the workers "ate like pigs and dogs and toiled like buffaloes and horses." They "worked until they were old, and their lot was worse than a blade of grass." They were oppressed politically, and their livelihood was uncertain. But the capitalists never worked.

They bossed the workers around and led extravagant and degenerate lives. Their wealth increased all the time. Why? Marx's theory of capital and surplus value revealed this secret and scientifically answered these questions. How did Marx's theory of capital and surplus value reveal the secret of the capitalists' exploitation of the workers? We must start from that special commodity, labor power.

Labor power means human work, the sum total of a person's physical and mental effort. In any society, labor power is the chief factor of production. But only in the capitalist society is labor power a commodity. There are two conditions under which labor power becomes a commodity. First, the laborer is a "free man." He is free to sell his labor power as a commodity. Second, the laborer has nothing aside from his labor.

He has no means of production or means of livelihood and must sell his labor power to live. These two conditions occurred when the feudal society collapsed and in the course of polarization between the small commodity producers and primitive accumulation. The employment of workers by the capitalist consists of buying their labor power and converting them into hired slaves.

Once labor power becomes a commodity, it possesses value and use value, like other commodities. The value of labor power, like the value of all commodities, is determined by the amount of socially necessary labor required for its production and reproduction. The capitalist must maintain the labor capacity of the worker if he wants him to work for him. To maintain the worker's labor capacity, it is necessary to feed, clothe, and shelter him and provide him with means of livelihood. Therefore, the value of labor power must include, first of all, the value of the means of livelihood needed to maintain his sustenance. At the same time, workers grow old and die. In order to maintain the capitalist exploitative system, the capitalist needs new workers as replacements. Therefore, the value of labor power must also include the value of means of livelihood needed by the worker to support his children and other dependents. To more fully exploit the worker, the capitalist generally requires him to master certain skills through general education and training. Thus, the value of labor power must also include the cost of education and training. But this amount to very little. In general, it can be said that the socially neces sary labor needed for the production of labor power is the socially necessary labor needed for the production of the above- mentioned means of livelihood. In other words, the value of labor power is the value of the means of livelihood needed to kee the worker alive and his offspring growing.

As for the use value of labor power, it is different from the use value of other commodities. Labor power is a special com modity. Its use value possesses a special characteristic. Wher the use value of other commodities, like food grains and clothing, is consumed, no new use value is created. But the use of this special commodity labor power, that is, the worker's work, can create value and, moreover, can create value which is higher than the value of the labor power itself. "When the capitalist purchases labor power, it is this augmented value in which he is interested." (1) This difference is called surplus value.

The Surplus Value Expropriated by the Capitalist Comes from the Exploitation of Workers

How then does surplus value arise? Let us examine concretely the production process of surplus value. After the purchase of labor power by the capitalist, he forces the worker to work in his factories to produce commodities. There are two aspects of capitalist production process. It is a labor process. It is also a value-augmenting process.

A labor process is the purposeful process by which people use certain labor to transform the labor object for human need The characteristic of the capitalist labor process is that the capitalist possesses means of production. The worker toils un* der the capitalist's orders while his labor products belong to the capitalist. The result of the capitalist labor process is the production of a certain use value capable of satisfying certain social needs. But that is not the purpose of capitalist production.

The capitalist allows the worker to produce certain use value only because use value is the material carrier of value. If he does not provide some use value, there will be no demand for his commodity, and the value (including surplus value) produced will not be realized.

The capitalist production process is also a value-augmenting process. When the workers produce use value, they are also using their active labor to create new value. The new value which the workers create is higher than the value of the labor power itself. This is called value-augmenting. This value - augmenting is the ultimate goal of the capitalist. The value - augmenting process is the major theme of the capitalist production process.

Take the example of cotton yarn production. The capitalist first purchases enough means of production for a worker's twelve-hour workday. Suppose the value of these means of production is equal to forty-eight hours of labor, totaling twenty - four yuan. He also purchases a day's labor power from a worker. Suppose the value of a day's labor power is equal to six hours of labor, totaling three yuan. Then the worker is made to spin yarn. Since what the capitalist has purchased is a day's labor power, he will not ask the worker to work for only six hours. Suppose the worker toils twelve hours a day. Then, the value of the cotton yarn produced is equal to sixty hours of labor, totaling thirty yuan, of which twenty-four yuan is transferred from the means of production and six yuan is the new value created by the worker in twelve hours' labor. In this labor process, the capitalist gets only twenty-seven yuan, of which twenty-four yuan are used for purchasing means of production and three yuan for paying wages. The remainder is three yuan. This is the augmented value created by the worker and expropriated by the capitalist. The process of value augmenting is the production process of surplus value.

What takes place above still follows the principle of equivalence in exchange. But value is augmented, and surplus value produced. The key of this process is that the capitalist obtains the right to use the labor power he has purchased. 'The use value of the labor power, that is, the labor itself, belongs just as little to the vendor as the use value of oil which has been sold belongs to the oil dealer. The owner of money has paid the daily value of labor power. Consequently, its use during the day, the whole day's labor, belongs to him. The daily sustenance of labor power only costs half a working day, although such labor power can be in action the entire day. Consequently the value which its employment creates in a single day is double its own daily value." (2) That the capitalist can build large factories and accumulate ever more wealth is due to the fact that the value created by labor is far larger than the value of labor power and the difference is expropriated by the capitalis Through the analysis of the production process of surplus value, we can see clearly that surplus value is created by worl ers in the production sphere. But to conceal the exploitation ol workers, the bourgeoisie and their agents insist that the new value obtained by the capitalist comes from the circulation sphere. We must thoroughly expose such lies. Surplus value cannot be explained by saying that the buyer buys commodities below their values or that the seller sells commodities above their values, since the gain or loss obtained through the transaction will be offset by the change in roles between buyers and sellers. Neither can surplus value be explained by deceit, because even though deception may increase the welfare of one party at the expense of another, it cannot increase the total wealth of both parties. "The whole capitalist class of a countrj cannot become richer by deceiving themselves." (3) If there ifl any relation between surplus value and the circulation sphere, it is the fact that the capitalist cannot divorce himself from tin circulation sphere in buying labor and selling commodities. In the circulation sphere, the capitalist buys labor power which provides the condition for producing surplus value. And the capitalist realizes this surplus value through selling his commodities. In any case, surplus value can only be created in the production sphere and not in the circulation sphere. Surplus value can only be the product of the capitalist's exploitation of the worker in the production process.

Once we understand the secret of capitalist exploitation, we can appreciate the nature of capital and the basic economic law under capitalism. Capital is a value that can bring about surplus value, or it can be said to be a value with self-value- augmenting power. Capital is not a simple thing. It expresses the capitalist mode of production, namely the class relations whereby the capitalist exploits the workers.

This relation expressed by capital is a result of historical development. Means of production and money existed before the emergence of the capitalist mode of production. But only under the capitalist mode of production when capital is owned by the capitalist and is used as a means to exploit the worker's surplus value does it become capital. Marx pointed out, "The Negro is simply a negro. Only under some conditions does he become a slave. A spinning machine is a machine for spinning cotton. Only under some conditions does it become capital."(4) Bourgeois economists insisted that the means of production is capital. According to this reasoning, the stone implements and wood clubs used by primitive man were capital. The purpose of their fallacies was to conceal the class relations among people with the relations among things, to conceal the nature of capitalist exploitation, to negate the fact that capital is a historical category, and to explain capitalism as eternal and existing from time immemorial.

Marx pointed out in his analysis of the capitalist mode of production that "to produce surplus value and to make money is the absolute law of this mode of production." (5) This law of surplus value is also the basic economic law of capitalism.

It reveals the objective purpose and nature of capitalism. There would be no capitalist production without the production of surplus value. All the activities of the capitalist are aimed at squeezing the sweat and blood from the worker for profit. The capitalist's greed for money is never satisfied and his thirst for surplus value is never quenched. This is the nature of the capitalist. "The purpose of capital is not to satisfy needs, but to produce profit." (6) "Capital and its increase in value are the beginning and the end of production and are the means and the end of production.'* (7) The whole capitalist system is base on the cruel exploitation of the worker by the capitalist. Capitalism is the evil system in which man exploits man.

To maintain the capitalist system and conceal the nature of capitalist exploitation, the bourgeoisie and their spokesmen fabricated all sorts of fallacies to deceive the masses. They said that the suffering of the workers was due to their "bad luck" and that the wealth of the capitalist was a result of their "diligence and thrift." These are all lies. The capitalist never works; how can he be "diligent"? He leads an extravagant and evil life; how can he be "thrifty"? In the old society, the suffering of the worker was not because of "bad luck," but because most of the products produced were expropriated by the capitalist. In short, the poverty of the worker and the wealth of the capitalist arose from the same source. It was the capitalist exploitative system based on the capitalist's private ownership.

The Cruel Means by Which the Capitalists Exploit and Oppress the Workers

The Rate of Surplus Value Reflects the Degree of Exploitation of the Worker by the Capitalist

The capitalist is capital in disguise. His soul is the soul of capital. The capitalist is a bloodsucker. He will not stop if there is still something left to be squeezed out of the worker. To get more surplus value, the capitalist tries his best to increase the exploitation of the worker. We can gauge the degree of the capitalist's exploitation of the worker by the rate of surplus value.

To understand the rate of surplus value as a gauge of the degree of the capitalist's exploitation of the worker, we must understand the different roles played by the means of production and labor power in the creation of value and in augmenting value and the difference between constant and variable capital.

Means of production is consumed in the process of production and loses its original value in use. But its value is not lost.

It is simply transferred to new products through the worker's labor. But this transfer cannot add any new value. Therefore, the part of capital which is used to buy means of production is called constant capital. In contrast to constant capital, the part of capital used by the capitalist to buy labor power is called variable capital because the new value created by labor exceeds the value the labor power received. Surplus value is the product of the augmenting of variable capital.

Let us use "c" to denote constant capital, "v" for variable capital, and "m" for surplus value. Then, the advance payment for capital is c 4· v and the total value of products is c + v + m. Since the value of c is unchanged in the production process, m is merely the result of the augmenting of v. So to indicate the degree of exploitation of the worker by the capitalist, we can ignore c and contrast only m with v. Then m/vis the rate of surplus value. Using the above example of spinning, v is three yuan, and m is also three yuan. The rate of surplus value reflecting the degree of exploitation by the capitalist is thus m/v, that is, 100 percent.

From the process of value-augmenting, we can see that the labor time of a workday can be divided into two parts: one is the value (wage) used to reproduce variable capital. That part of labor time is needed for the sustenance of the worker and is called necessary labor time. The other part is used to produce surplus value for the capitalist and is called surplus labor. Therefore, the rate of surplus value can also be expressed as:

$$\text{rate of surplus value} = \frac{surplus\ value\ (m)}{variable\ capital\ (v)} = \frac{surplus\ labor\ time}{necessary\ labor\ time}$$

To Obtain Absolute Surplus Value through Lengthening Labor Time

The capitalist always tries to increase the rate of surplus value by increasing the exploitation of the worker. In order to increase the rate of surplus value, the capitalist generally resorts to lengthening labor time. Under capitalism, the labor time of a worker in a day is the sum of necessary labor and surplus labor time. Under the condition of constant necessary labor time, the longer the labor time, the longer the surplus labor time. If, in the beginning, the daily labor time of a worker is twelve hours, six hours of which are necessary labor time, then six hours are surplus labor time. Now the capitalist extends the labor time to fifteen hours. With necessary labor time constant at six hours, surplus labor time becomes nine hours, three hours more than before. Thus, the ratio between surplus labor time and necessary labor time changes from six to six to nine to six. And the rate of surplus value is increased from 100 percent to 150 percent. This surplus value produced by the absolute lengthening of the daily labor time is called absolute surplus value.

In old China, the working time of the worker was incredibly long. The daily labor time was 15, 16 or even more than 18 hours. It was not unusual for a worker "to see stars in the sky before he went to bed late at night and to see stars when he had to get up early the next morning." Prior to liberation, the workers in San-t'iao-shih, Tientsin, had to work 357 days a year and about 20 hours a day. Reckoning on the basis of 8 hours a day, it was equivalent to working 893 workdays. One year's labor was equivalent to nearly 3 years. To lengthen the labor time of the workers, the capitalists thought up all kinds of restrictions, such as 10 minutes for meals and registration before going to toilets. They even resorted to the mean trick of setting the clock back! The longer the worker's labor time, the longer the surplus labor time and the longer the absolute surplus value obtained by the capitalist. Under the cruel exploitation of the capitalist, this constant physical exhaustion severely strained the worker, often resulting in early death.

Though the lengthening of labor time by the capitalist to increase exploitation is an easy method, it inevitably leads to opposition from the worker. At the same time, the capitalist cannot extend the work time to twenty-four hours a day because there is a physical limit to labor power expenditure. Thus, the capitalist adopts another, more obscure method by shortening the necessary labor time and thus lengthening the relative surplus labor time to increase his exploitation of the worker.

To Extract Relative Surplus Value through Shortening the Necessary Labor Time

How can the necessary labor time be shortened? We know that the necessary labor time is the labor time needed for the reproduction of the value of labor power. And the value of labor power is determined by the value of necessary means of liveli - hood for the sustenance of the worker and his dependents. If the capitalist adopts new techniques and new machines to increase general labor productivity and thus reduce the value of means of livelihood necessary for the reproduction of labor power, then, even if the total daily labor time of the worker is constant, the relative surplus labor time can be lengthened because the necessary labor time can now be shortened because the value of labor power is reduced. Suppose the original necessary labor time is six hours and the surplus labor time is also six hours. Now, if the general labor productivity has been doubled, the value of the means of livelihood necessary for the worker and his dependents will be reduced by half, and the labor time necessary for reproducing the labor power value will also be shortened from six to three hours. And the surplus labor time will be lengthened from six to nine hours, three hours more than before. The ratio of surplus labor time to necessary labor time changes from six to six to nine to three. The rate of surplus value increases from 100 percent to 300 percent.

This surplus value created by the shortening of the necessary labor time and the relative lengthening of the surplus labor time is called relative surplus value.

It must also be pointed out that the efforts of the individual capitalist to adopt new techniques and new machines to force the worker to increase his labor productivity cannot reduce the value of means of livelihood. Therefore, he cannot immediately fulfill his aim of extracting relative surplus value. If this is the case, why does the capitalist adopt new techniques and new machines? The direct motive of the capitalist for adopting new techniques and new machines is to reduce the individual labor time for commodity production below the socially necessary labor time, so that when he sells his commodities at values determined by the socially necessary labor time he can get more surplus value than other capitalists. The surplus value resulting from lower individual labor time of commodities than the socially necessary labor time is called excess surplus labor. But the capitalist who first adopts new techniques is not likely to enjoy this excess surplus value for long because of similar actions by other capitalists to share part of the excess profit. When the new techniques and new machines have been widely adopted and the general labor productivity elevated, the value of commodities will come down. The gap between individual labor time and socially necessary labor time leading to excess surplus value will disappear. Excess surplus value will also disappear. However, as a result, general labor productivity will have been elevated. The values of many commodities will come down, and the means of livelihood constituting the value of labor will be cheaper. The value of labor power will be cheaper, and the necessary labor time will be shortened. Consequently, the capitalist can extract more relative surplus labor.

The greedy capitalist not only resorts to elevating labor productivity to increase his relative surplus value, he also resorts to shortening the necessary labor time by increasing labor intensity to extract more relative surplus value. Marx said: "In a sense, the elevation of labor productivity and the increase of labor intensity serve the same function. They will increase the total production derived from a given period of time. Consequently, they will shorten the part of the workday needed for the production of the workers' own means of livelihood or other equivalents." (8) The capitalist quickens the operation of machines, raises the labor quota, and reduces total employment but not total workload to increase the labor intensity of the worker. The labor of the worker is ever more demanding.

After one day T s work, he is completely exhausted. Take the example of the Shanghai Shen-hsin Yarn Mill. In 1933, 440 workers were employed for every 100,000 spindles. In order to compete with the Japanese-operated yarn mills and to get more surplus value, the capitalists of this mill forced up labor intensity by reducing the number of workers. In 1934, only 270 workers were employed for 100,000 spindles. In the old society under the oppression of the capitalist, the workers were so overworked that many became senile at age forty.

Depress Wages below the Value of Labor to Extract More Surplus Value

The tricks adopted by the capitalist to exploit the worker are numerous. He often depresses and deducts wages. When we analyzed absolute surplus value earlier, we assumed that the capitalist pays wages according to the value of labor power.

But the wages of the worker are often below the value of his labor power. The capitalist tries his best to depress the worker's wages. Even though the worker's wages may barely be enough for his sustenance, he still tries to make all sorts of reductions to depress wages below the value of labor power so that even a minimum level of subsistence cannot be maintained by the worker. For example, there was a regulation in K'ai-luan Coal Mine: forty-seven cents daily for the mule as fodder, but not more than twenty-two cents daily for the miner in wages. "Men were inferior to mules." Also, in old China, many plants had penal codes for the workers, with all sorts of fancy items. Sometimes, the fine was even higher than the wage. For example, emptying water indiscriminately was punishable; looking out of the window was also punishable; assembling and associating were even more punishable. All the fines finally ended up in the capitalist's pockets as an additional source of income.

The capitalist employed a large number of women and child laborers to engage in more cruel exploitation. With the employment of a large number of women and child laborers, the worker's wages were often reduced to below the value of labor power.

The wages of women and child laborers were even lower. In old China, women worked for more than ten hours daily, just like men, but their wages were only two-thirds or half that of men. The wages for child laborers were even lower, often only half that of women. Some capitalists merely provided some cheap meals with no money wage. The capitalist treated the 'Young apprentices" and the "child laborers" as less than human. Marx pointed out that the capitalist "extracts silk out of the blood of children who are so young that they have to be helped to their workshop." (9) Children in the growing stage and at school age were underfed, underclothed, and tortured by the capitalist. They were often beaten up and cursed. A large number of child laborers perished under the cruel exploitation of the capitalist.

In capitalist society, the capitalist not only cruelly exploited the worker, he also ruthlessly oppressed him. In old China, many capitalists stipulated plant regulations to oppress the worker. The tens or even a hundred penalty code items stripped much of the worker's freedom. Examples were "searching before and after work" and "the management has the right to fire workers." The plants were like prisons, and the workers were like prisoners. Some capitalists even had military and police forces stationed in the plant to oppress the workers.

Capitalism brought untold suffering to the worker. It is an evil, exploitative system. But renegade Liu Shao-ch'i tried his best to defend the capitalist exploitative system and advocated that "exploitation has its merits." He even said, "Capitalist exploitation is not only not evil, it has its merits." This is all nonsense! Marx's theory of surplus value is the most eloquent criticism of that so-called "exploitation has its merits." Liu Shao-ch'i and company's vain attempt to restore the capitalist exploitative system in socialist China could only expose their evil countenance as the spokesmen of the bourgeoisie.

<u>Wages Conceal the Exploitative Relation of Capitalism</u>

Wages Are a Disguised Form of the Value or Price of Labor

In capitalist society, the worker toiled in the capitalist's plant and earned wages from the capitalist. The worker received a day's wages after he toiled for a day. He received a week's wages after he toiled for a week. On the surface, it looked as if all his labor had been compensated and that it was an "equivalent exchange." In fact, the form of wages concealed the exploitation of the worker by the capitalist.

Marx pointed out: 'Wages are not what they appear to be. They are not the value or price of labor, but a disguised form of the value or price of labor power." (10) The wages advocated by the capitalist as "the value or price of labor" are entirely fictitious.

The key lies in the distinction between labor power and labor. This "involves an extremely important question in political economy." (11) Under the capitalist system, what is being sold and bought as a commodity is labor power, not labor.

Why is labor not a commodity and why can it not be bought or sold? This is because, first, if labor is a commodity, it should exist before it is sold, just like other commodities. But, in fact, labor is the exercise of labor power. It does not exist before it is sold. It exists only after it is sold and used in the labor process. Also, once the worker's labor is hired out, it no longer belongs to the worker himself. His labor belongs to the capitalist. Second, if labor is a commodity, according to the requirements of the law of value, it must be exchanged for equivalent value. Then the capitalist should pay the worker the full value created by the worker as his wage and as payment for the worker's labor. If this were the case, then the capitalist would lose his source of wealth and surplus value would be abolished. There would no longer be capitalism. Third, if labor is a commodity, it should have a value. How should this value be determined? We know that the value of all commodities is determined by the amount of embodied labor. If the value of labor is also determined by the amount of labor, the result is to evaluate labor with labor. This is a tautology.

From this we can see that labor is not a commodity. It has no value. There is no such thing as "the value or price of labor."

Under capitalism, the capitalist purchases labor power from the worker, but not labor. The wage paid to the worker by the capitalist is equivalent only to the value of the labor power. The remainder of what the worker's labor creates over and above the value of the labor power is surplus value which is exploited by the capitalist. Therefore, the capitalist wage reflects the relation between the hiring capitalist and the hired worker, between the exploiting capitalist and the exploited worker.

The Downward Trend of the Real Wage of the Worker

The capitalist usually pays wages in money form. When the worker sells his labor power, he obtains a certain amount of money. The wage expressed in money form is called the nominal wage. The amount of money cannot reflect the actual standard of living of the worker. The real standard of living can only be reflected by the amount of means of livelihood purchasable by the money wage. This wage that reflects the real standard of living of the worker is called the real wage.

The nominal wage and the real wage are not always the same.

With the nominal wage held constant, the real wage can decline. When the purchasing power of money declines and the prices of the means of livelihood go up, the same amount of the nominal wage can only be exchanged for a smaller amount of means of livelihood. Then the real wage falls. Sometimes even if the nominal wage goes up a bit, but less than the increase in prices of the means of livelihood, the real wage will still decline.

In capitalist society, there is a downward trend in the real

wage of the worker. The bourgeoisie always use inflation, price increases, and rent hikes to increase the gap between the nominal and the real wage and to exploit the worker.

In old China, "wages increased at a snail's pace while prices went up like a balloon." To maintain their reactionary rule and plunder the people, the Chiang [Kai-shek] dynasty quickened the operation of the money printing press. In the twelve years between 1937 and 1949, the issue of notes increased by 140,000 million times and the price index increased by 8,500,000 million times. The worker in old China had more than his share of suffering from inflation. On the eve of the collapse of the Chiang dynasty, on every payday "the price of rice jumped three times while one trudged across the street." In old China, the worker not only was paid a low wage, but what he could buy with it was even less. The wage was not worth a damn. It was almost impossible to support a family. Sometimes after strikes the nominal wage might go up a little, but prices went up a lot more. The lot of the worker was getting worse every day. What was even worse, the rents were very high. Even a run-down thatched shed cost a fortune. Marx and Engels pointed out, "After the exploitation by the plant owner, another group of bourgeoisie — landlords, proprietors, and pawn shop owners — were waiting to take turns getting their shares from the worker's wages."(12)

The Working Class Struggles against Capitalist Exploitation

The decline in the real wage reduced the majority of workers to cold and starvation. The working class naturally rose to oppose capitalist exploitation.

The economic struggle which the working class undertook to increase wages in order to protect their right to survive and to oppose the cruel exploitation of the bourgeoisie was very significant. This was because it not only delayed the decline of real wages, but it was also able to strengthen the unity of the working class, elevate their class consciousness, and temper their combat spirit. But we must not exaggerate the significance of economic struggle. Marx pointed out that the working class "should not forget: in this daily struggle they are only opposing the effect, but not the cause that produces this effect; they are only delaying the downward trend, not changing the direction of the trend; they are only suppressing the symptom, not curing the disease." (13) Therefore, if the working class wants an ultimate solution, it cannot limit itself to economic struggles but must also extend from economic struggles to political struggles, overthrow the reactionary rule of the bourgeoisie, and demolish the capitalist exploitative system.

However, all sorts of scabs advocated: It is only necessary to engage in economic struggles. According to their fallacies, there is no need for the working class to seize political power through violent revolution and demolish the capitalist system.

It should be contented with a little wage increase and some improvement in working conditions. These fallacies peddled by a handful of scabs were intended to vainly lead the proletarian revolutionary movement to the stray path of bourgeois reformism. They wanted the working class to serve as the capitalists' hired slaves forever. "Workers should not abide by the conservative motto 'a fair day's wage for a fair day's labor!'

They should write on their banner the revolutionary slogan:

Do away with the system of hired labor! (14)

Major Study References

Marx, Capital, Vol. 1, Chapters 4, 5, 10, 17.

Marx, Wage Labor and Capital.

Marx, Wage, Prices and Profit.

Chairman Mao, "The Analysis of Chinese Social Classes." Chairman, Mao, "The Chinese Revolution and the Chinese Communist Party," Chapter 1, Section 3; Chapter 2, Section 4.

Review Problems

1. How does surplus value arise? Why do we say that the production of surplus value is the nature of capitalist production?
2. What methods does the capitalist use to exploit and oppress the worker?
3. Why do we say that the capitalist wage is merely a disguised form of the value or price of labor power?
4. Why do we have to learn Marx's theory of surplus value?

How do we use Marx's theory of surplus value to criticize Liu Shao‑ch'i and company's viewpoint that "exploitation has its merit"?

Notes

1) Marx, Capital, Vol. 1, Compl ete Works of Marx and Engels, Vol. 23, p. 219.
2) Ibid.
3) Ibid., pp. 185‑186.
4) Marx, Wage Labor and Capital, Selected Works of Mar x and Engels, Vol. 1, Jen‑min ch'u‑pan‑she, 1972, p.362.
5) Marx, Capital, Vol. 1, Complete Works of Marx and Engels, Vol. 23, p. 679.
6) Marx, Capital, Vol. 3, Jen‑min ch'u‑pan‑she, 1966, p. 280.
7) Ibid., p. 272.
8) Marx, Capital, Vol. 1, C omp lete Wor ks of Ma rx an d Engels, Vol. 23, p. 578.
9) Ibid., p. 325.
10) Marx, Critique of the Gotha Program, Selected Works of Marx and Engels, Vol. 3, Jen‑min ch'u‑pan‑she, 1972, p. 17.
11) Engels, "Introduction to Wage Labor and Capital, " Selected Works of Marx and Engels, Vol. 1, Jen‑min ch'u‑pan‑ she, 1972, p. 341.
12) Communist Manifesto, Selected Works of Marx and Engels, Vol. 1, Jen‑min ch'u‑pan‑she, 1972, pp. 258‑259.
13) Marx, Wage, Prices and Profit, S elected Works of Marx and Engels, Vol. 2, Jen‑min ch'u‑pan‑she, 1972, p.203.
14) Ibid., pp. 203‑204.

5. The Widening Gap between the Rich and the Poor in Capitalist Society

Capital Accumulation and the Impoverishment of the Working Class

The capitalist tries his best to extract absolute and relative surplus value and to convert it into capital for the exploitation and oppression of the worker on a larger scale. This process of converting surplus value into capital is called capital accumulation. The analysis of capital accumulation makes us realize why in the old society the capitalist who never labored was getting richer and the toiling worker's lot was getting worse.

It helps us further understand why the expropriation of the expropriator, the extinction of capitalism, and the inevitable triumph of socialism cannot be reversed by any reactionary forces and why the overthrow of the evil capitalist system is the great historical mission of the proletariat.

Capital Accumulation Increases the Exploitation of the Workers

Analyze Capitalist Simple Reproduction and Expose the Lie That the Capitalist Supports the Worker

We said earlier that the conversion of surplus value expropriated by the capitalist into capital is capital accumulation. Before we analyze capital accumulation, let us see what would happen if the capitalist spent the expropriated surplus value all on himself instead of converting it to capital. Under this condition, the production of the capitalist could not be expanded.

He could only carry on capitalist simple reproduction. Suppose a capitalist started a plant with 10,000 yuan, of which 8,000 yuan was used to buy the plant building, raw materials, and machine equipment (to simplify the example, suppose this 8,000 yuan of means of production was totally expended in the year with its value transferred to the products) and 2,000 yuan was used to purchase labor power. Further, suppose the rate of surplus value was 100 percent. Then the value of annual products would be equal to $8,000c + 2,000v + 2,000m = 12,000$ yuan, of which, 2,000 yuan would be surplus value. If the capitalist spent this 2,000 yuan of surplus value on luxury consumption for himself and his family dependents, the capital in the capitalist's hands at the beginning of the second year would still be $8,000c + 2,000v = 10,000$ yuan. If there were no change in the surplus value, the value of the second year's products would still be $8,000c + 2,000v + 2,000m = 12,000$ yuan. In the course of reproduction, the scale of operation would not have expanded, staying at the original level. This reproduction based on the original scale is called simple reproduction.

What does capitalist simple reproduction explain?

First, we can clearly see who supports whom in the capitalist society. If we look at it from one single production process, it looks as if the capitalist supports the worker by advancing his capital as wages. This is how the capitalist puts it. But, if we look at it from the reproduction process, the capitalist's lie is easily exposed. Wages are only part of the value created by the worker himself in the production process. In the value newly created by the worker is included not only the value for the support of the worker himself and the reproduction of labor power, but also the surplus value for the support of the capitalist and for his extravagant living. Therefore, it is not the capitalist who supports the worker. On the contrary, it is the worker who supports the capitalist.

Second, from the process of simple reproduction, we can see

that the capital of the capitalist is converted from surplus value. Using our earlier example, this capitalist who started out with 10,000 yuan spent 2,000 yuan on his personal consumption. Thus, after five years, his initial capital would have been completely spent. But, through simple reproduction, after five years he still had 10,000 yuan as capital. This 10,000 yuan was no longer the capital he started out with, but the sum total of his continual extraction of surplus value in five years. Marx said, 'Ignoring all accumulation, the simple continuation of the production process or simple reproduction would, after a longer or shorter period of time, transform any capital into accumulated capital or capitalized surplus value." (1)

Since the capital of the capitalist is converted from surplus value created by the worker, it is entirely reasonable that all means of production expropriated from the capitalist should belong to the proletarian state if the working class has seized political power. This is merely taking back the wealth created by the labor of the ancestors of the working class.

Finally, from the process of simple reproduction, we can also see that capitalist reproduction not only reproduces various commodities, but also reproduces the capitalist production relations. In the process of reproduction, the worker continuously produces the variable capital used for the purchase of labor power. When the production process ends, the worker is still an empty-handed hired laborer, and the capitalist still possesses all the means for the exploitation of the worker.

The Capitalist Expands Reproduction for the Sake of Extracting More Surplus Value

We assumed above that the capitalist spent all the surplus value on his personal consumption. Because of this, reproduction could only be carried on at the original scale. But, simple reproduction is not the characteristic of capitalist production.

The characteristic of capitalist production is expanded reproduction.

To carry on expanded reproduction, the capitalist cannot spend all the expropriated surplus value on personal consumption. He must spare part of it for conversion into capital to buy new machines and equipment and to hire additional workers before he can expand the scale of operation and realize expanded reproduction.

Suppose the capitalist started out with 10,000 yuan, of which 8,000 yuan was constant capital and 2,000 yuan was variable capital, and that the rate of surplus value was 100 percent. When the production process was completed, the value of products would be $8,000c + 2,000v$

+ 2,000m = 12,000 yuan. Further, suppose that the capitalist used half of the 2,000 yuan of surplus value for personal consumption and the other half for accumulation to be converted into capital. If the proportion between constant capital and variable capital were kept constant, then from this 1,000 yuan of new capital, 800 yuan would go into constant capital, and 200 yuan into variable capital. In the second year, the total amount of capital would be increased to 11,000 yuan. Its composition would be 8,800c + 2,200v + 2,200m = 13,200 yuan. Compared with the value of the first year's products of 12,000 yuan, this capitalist realized expanded reproduction.

From capitalist expanded reproduction, we can see that expanded production can be carried out only because part of the surplus value has been converted into capital. If, under the condition of simple reproduction, the capital invested by the capitalist can be seen as converted from surplus value only after a period of time, then under the condition of expanded reproduction, the added capital can be seen as converted from surplus value right from the beginning.

Why does the capitalist not spend all of the surplus value on his personal consumption but instead carry out capital accumulation for expanded reproduction? Some bourgeois economists explained capital accumulation as the virtue of "abstinence" on the part of the capitalist, as if capital accumulation by the capitalist were for the good of society as a whole and involved a restraint of his consumption desire.

Marx exposed the nature of "abstinence." Marx pointed out that the capitalist possessed "an absolute desire to get rich." (2) The greed of the capitalist for surplus value is limitless. Surplus value can be increased continuously only if the capitalist continuously accumulates capital, increases the amount of capital, and expands the scale of production. At the same time, capitalist competition also forces him to accumulate capital. Whoever has more capital is in an advantageous position with respect to the addition of equipment, the purchase of raw materials, and the adoption of new techniques. He is also more likely to increase labor productivity and to depress the individual labor time of a commodity below the socially necessary labor time, so as to triumph in the competition. If the reverse were the case, he would fail in the competition and be swallowed up by the bigger capitalist. Competition becomes a source of pressure on every capitalist. The fear of failure and bankruptcy in competition forces the capitalist to engage in capital accumulation to strengthen his competitive power. "Competition transforms the internal law of capitalist production into a coercive external law governing every capitalist. Competition forces the capitalist to maintain his capital by expanding it continuously. And he expands his capital by progressive accumulation." (3)

It can be seen that it is not "abstinence" but greed and fear which motivate the capitalist to convert part of the surplus value extracted from the worker into capital. The more the capitalist exploits, the larger the accumulated capital. The larger the accumulated capital, the more surplus value can be exploited. Therefore, capital accumulation is not only a result of the exploitation of the worker, but also a means by which the capitalist extends and expands his exploitation of the worker.

The Unemployment of Workers Is the Inevitable Result of Capital Accumulation

The Increase in the Organic Composition of Capital Leads to the Expulsion of the Worker by Machines

The process of capital accumulation is not only a process of increasing the total amount of capital. In this process, there is also the change in the composition of capital and the consequent adverse effect on the proletariat.

From the material side, the composition of capital is expressed as the proportion between means of production (plant, machines, equipment, raw materials) and labor power. There is a definite relation between the amount of means of production purchased and the number of workers employed. For example, there is a definite number of spindles a worker can manage using a certain amount of cotton each day. The level of this proportion depends on the technological level of production in society, the characteristics of various production spheres, and the degree of mechanization. It also depends on the technical equipment of various enterprises. Therefore, we can call this proportion the technical composition of capital.

The composition of capital can also be viewed from the value viewpoint. The value of means of production is expressed as constant capital, and the value of labor power is expressed as variable capital. The proportion between constant and variable capital is called the value composition of capital.

There is a close relation between the technical and value composition of capital. In general, the value composition of capital varies with the technical composition of capital. 'The value composition of capital, which is determined by the technical composition of capital and which reflects its change, is called the organic composition of capital." (4) The formula for the organic composition of capital is c : v. For example, suppose a capitalist has 10,000 yuan, of which 8,000 yuan is constant capital and 2,000 yuan is variable capital. Then the organic composition of capital is 8,000c : 2,000v, that is, 4: 1.

In the course of the development of capitalism, the organic composition of capital is not constant. To extract more surplus value and to gain an upper hand in competition, the capitalist must improve the technical equipment of the enterprise by substituting machines for hand labor or new machines for old machines. Thus, the capitalist must increase his capital in machine equipment. The substitution of machines for labor enables the worker to produce even more products in a given period of time with an even higher consumption of raw materials. The capitalist must also increase his capital for the purchase of more raw materials. Thus, with the continual accumulation of capital, the proportion of constant capital in the total capital constantly increases. On the other hand, the proportion of variable capital gets smaller all the time, leading to an increase in the organic composition of capital.

In general, the precondition for the increase in the organic composition of capital is the increase in individual capital. Capital can be increased in two forms: one is by capital accumulation, that is, an increase in the total amount of capital by the accumulation of individual capital; the other is by capital concentration, that is, the absorption of small capital by big capital through competition or the merger of several companies into a joint-stock corporation so that capital that was once scattered is concentrated into larger capital. Capital accumulation and capital concentration inevitably increase the organic composition of capital.

The increase in organic composition of capital has serious repercussions for the working class. If the organic composition of capital is constant, the accumulation of capital will increase the corresponding demand for labor power. That is, it will correspondingly increase the employment opportunities of the worker. But after the organic composition of capital is increased, the result of capital accumulation is no longer the same. It can increase the total demand for labor power. But this increase will be much smaller than the increase in constant capital. Under certain conditions, the total demand for labor power may even be lower than before. This is because the demand for labor power does not depend on the size of total capital but on the size of variable capital. For example, when the organic composition of capital is 4 :1, it means that for every 100 yuan of total capital, 20 yuan can be used for hiring workers. But when the organic composition of capital is increased to 9:1, it means that for every 100 yuan, only 10 yuan is available for hiring workers. Thus, even if the total capital increases from 10,000 yuan to 15,000 yuan, the amount of variable capital decreases from 2,000 yuan to 1,500 yuan. This demonstrates that the increase in the organic composition of capital reduces employment opportunities for the worker. In the capitalist society, the working class creates machines. But when the machines are used by the capitalist, a large number of workers are displaced and unemployed. The adoption of sewing machines by the capitalist led to the unemployment of many sewing workers. The adoption of packing machines led to the unemployment of many packing workers. The adoption of typesetting machines led to the unemployment of many typesetting workers. In the development process of capitalism, with the improvement in techniques and the increase in the organic composition of capital, employment opportunities for the laborers are correspondingly reduced and unemployment increases.

This is called the expulsion of workers by machines.

Relative Surplus Population Is the Inevitable Outcome of Capital Accumulation

The increase in the organic composition of capital relatively reduces the demand for labor power. But in the course of capital accumulation, the supply of labor power increases absolutely. With the development of capitalist production techniques and the widespread adoption of machines, many labor operations were so simplified that many women and children could join the ranks of hired labor. At the same time, in the course of capital accumulation, a large number of small commodity producers and small capitalists went bankrupt and had to sell their labor power to support themselves. The development of capitalism in the countryside also brought bankruptcy to a large number of peasants who flocked to the city to earn their living. All these factors contributed to an absolute increase in the supply of labor power.

Thus, on the one hand, the demand for labor power was reduced relatively. On the other hand, the supply of labor power increased absolutely. In the end, there always exists in the capitalist society a large body of unemployed, resulting in a relative surplus in population.

The so-called relative surplus population is "surplus" only in relation to the capital demand for it. It does not imply that the population is in absolute surplus such that it can no longer be supported by the means of livelihood produced by society. In fact, there is no such thing as an absolute population surplus because a person not only has a mouth that can consume food grain, but also two hands that can create certain material wealth. Once the laboring masses control their own destiny, they can advance toward the depth and width of production to create ever more means of livelihood for a more diversified life. Only in the capitalist society, where the laborers cannot control their own destiny and the machines created by them are used as capital, are the workers displaced as relative surplus population. Therefore, Marx called the relative surplus population an outcome of "a special law of population under the capitalist mode of production." He pointed out, "Surplus worker population is an inevitable outcome of accumulation or the development of wealth on the capitalist basis." (5)

There are three basic forms of surplus population in the capitalist society:

First, mobile surplus population. This refers to the unemployed population which has been temporarily displaced in the production process. This kind of unemployment is most common in industrial centers. In time of crises and after new machines and new techniques are adopted, some workers will be displaced. But in time of recovery and when industry further develops, many of these unemployed workers will be absorbed back into factories. Very few workers in capitalist countries can escape from unemployment at one time or another. Most people are employed off and on.

Second, disguised surplus population, that is, surplus population in the countryside. After agricultural production has become capitalist and with the increase in the organic composition of capital, the demand for agricultural workers decreases steadily. Moreover, in agriculture this displacement of labor power is absolute. Unless new land is reclaimed, no additional labor power can be absorbed. Some of the laborers displaced by capitalist agriculture drift to the city. Others still cling to a small piece of land and barely support themselves by intensive cultivation and doing odd jobs. They may not be unemployed in form, but they are actually surplus in agricultural production. This is called disguised surplus population.

Third, static surplus population. These people perform household chores and do odd jobs. Though still belonging to the current labor force, their jobs are not stable. Their jobs often involve long hours and low wages. Their standard of living is depressed below the average level for the working class.

In the capitalist society, in addition to the above three kinds of surplus population, there is a large number of very poor people who depend on welfare and begging for their livelihood. Among them are the aged, the weak, the handicapped, the orphaned, and vagabonds who have lost their labor capacity. They constitute the lowest stratum of the relative surplus population, and their lot is the worst.

Relative surplus population is an inevitable outcome of capital accumulation. At the same time, these people become the lever of capital accumulation, or even a condition for the existence and development of the capitalist mode of production. The capitalist uses the existence of the unemployed workers as a trump card to increase oppression and exploitation of the currently employed. From the mouth of the capitalist, one can often hear such vicious words as, 'It is more difficult to find a hundred dogs than to find a hundred workers." Why is the capitalist so ferocious? Because outside the door of the plant there are thousands and thousands of unemployed workers. They are used by the capitalist to threaten the workers inside the plant and to depress their wages. At the same time, capitalism develops amidst competition and chaos and is characterized by sudden contractions and expansions. When production suddenly expands, the capitalist's demand for labor cannot be met by the natural increase of labor power. The capitalist requires a labor power "reservoir." Relative surplus population provides such a "reservoir." In this sense, we call the huge army of unemployed in capitalist society an industrial reserve army. It is required by the existence and development of the capitalist mode of production.

Malthus's "An Essay on the Principle of Population" Is a Reactionary Fallacy in Defense of Capitalism

In the capitalist society, the widespread existence of a huge army of unemployed is a "good" thing for the capitalist because it is conducive to exploitation. But it is also a shameful thing because it makes the so-called civilized country look very uncivilized. To remedy this situation, some intellectuals in the service of the bourgeoisie racked their brains to produce biased theories for the defense of the capitalist system. In the early nineteenth century, the reactionary An Essay on the Principle of Population cooked up by a vulgar English economist named Malthus was one such biased theory.

Malthus advanced a notorious argument. He said that population increases by the geometric progression (1, 2, 4, 8...), while the means of livelihood increases by the arithmetic progression (1, 2, 3, 4...). He argued that this is the basic reason for surplus population, unemployment, and poverty among the masses. This contention was intended to explain that unemployment and poverty are not the evils of the capitalist system, but a result of the law of Nature. According to Malthus's theory, wars and plagues are a blessing to human society. In wars and plagues, a large number of people die, thus ameliorating the effects of surplus population and rendering the increase in population more compatible with the increase in the means of livelihood.

Facts are stronger than arguments. Malthus's reactionary An Essay on the Principle of Popu l ation does not hold water. How did the pseudoscience that purported to show the geometric increase of population and the arithmetical increase of the means of livelihood come into being? What really happened was that Malthus took the increase in population in America in one period as the basis for his rate of population increase. He also took the increase in food production for one period in France as the basis for his rate of increase in the means of livelihood. The rapid increase in the American population at that time was not mainly due to the natural multiplication of population, but to other factors such as immigration. As to the food production of France, if it was compared with the increase of population in France and not with the increase of population in America, then it did not lag behind the increase in population, but exceeded the increase in population. In 1760, the population of France was 2.1 million. The average output of food grain per capita was 450 liters. Eighty years later in 1840, the population of France increased to 3.4 million, an increase of 62 percent. But the increase in food production was even faster. In 1840, the average output of food grain per capita was 832 liters, an increase of 85 percent. The data of many other capitalist countries also showed that the increase in population did not exceed the increase in the means of livelihood. On the contrary, the increase in the means of livelihood exceeded the increase in population. But, even so, the laboring people were very poor, and their lot miserable. Malthus's defense of the evils of the capitalist system by means of the so-called absolute surplus population was a futile effort.

The pernicious influence of Malthus's An Essay on the Principle of Population was widespread in the old China. Imperialists and Kuomintang reactionaries all along used Malthus's An Essay on the Principle of Population as a tool to oppose the Chinese people's revolution. Prior to the liberation, they uttered nonsense like the Chinese people were poor because there were too many of them, and they attempted to blame Nature for the evils of imperialism, feudalism, and bureaucratic capitalism. On the eve of the national liberation, they again talked nonsense, complaining that China had too many people. According to them, the people's government could not solve the food problem and would not last more than a few months. Chairman Mao sternly refuted this reactionary fallacy. He said, "The large population of China is a good thing. We know how to handle an even larger population. The solution is in production "devolution plus production can solve the food problem." (6) The experience of socialist China since its establishment has completely vindicated Chairman Mao's scientific judgment. Under the guidance of Chairman Mao's revolutionary line, unemployment has been eliminated in China. The socialist economy flourishes, and the people's standard of living steadily increases. A poor and backward China has established a socialist country on its way to prosperity and growth. The imperialist fallacies went thoroughly bankrupt.

Capital Accumulation Leads to the Impoverishment of the Proletariat

The Polarization between the Rich and the Poor Is a General Law of Capitalist Accumulation

Capital accumulation has entirely different consequences for the bourgeoisie and the proletariat. To the bourgeoisie, the process of capital accumulation is the process of capital addition and concentration and a process of the bourgeoisie's wealth expansion. To the proletariat, the process of capital accumulation is a process whereby "machines displace workers," and a process whereby the ranks of the unemployed are swollen, the employed workers are subject to increasing exploitation, and the living conditions of the whole working class worsen steadily. The polarization between the rich and the poor in capitalist society during capital accumulation will not shift according to human will. On one end of society is wealth accumulation; on the other is poverty accumulation. Marx pointed out, "This is an absolute and general law of capitalist accumulation." (7)

The revelation of this law by Marx is very significant. It tells us that the working and living conditions of the proletariat are determined by the capitalist production relations. Under the capitalist system, the development of production will only lead to the impoverishment of the proletariat. This impoverishment is not only relative but also absolute.

The Steadily Declining Share of the Proletariat in the National Income Leads to Relative Impoverishment

National income is the sum total of the newly created value of the whole society in one year. In capitalist society, national income is first divided into the part that goes to the workers' wages and the part that is plundered by the capitalists as surplus value. In the development of capitalism, what will happen to the income shares that go to the workers and to the capitalists respectively?

National income is wholly created by the laborers and increases steadily in the process of expanded reproduction. Under capitalism, the share of wages received by the proletariat steadily declines, and the share of surplus value received by the bourgeoisie steadily increases. This phenomenon is called the relative impoverishment of the proletariat. According to figures published by the United States government, the share of wages of American workers in the national income was 45.6 percent in 1843, 43.5 percent in 1866, 42.7 percent in 1891, 37 percent in 1938, 33.3 percent in 1945, and 29.7 percent in 1956. From these figures, we can see that with capital accumulation, the income of the workers declined steadily in relative terms, while the wealth expropriated by the bourgeoisie increased steadily.

The Steady Deterioration of Labor Conditions and Living Conditions Leads to the Absolute Impoverishment of the Proletariat

In capitalist society, there exists not only the relative impoverishment of the proletariat, but also their absolute impoverishment. This is what Lenin pointed out: "The impoverishment of the workers is absolute. That is to say, they become poorer and poorer, their lives more miserable, their meals worse, and their stomachs less full. And they have to be crowded into basements and attics." (8)

The major manifestations of the absolute impoverishment of the proletariat are as follows:

First, the existence of a large number of unemployed workers. Unemployment is the constant threat faced by the worker in a capitalist country. Once he is unemployed, he loses his source of income. His livelihood becomes a serious problem. This is an important indicator of the deterioration of the material living conditions of the proletariat. In the United States, the number of unemployed in 1945 was 1.1 million; in 1955, 2.654 million; in 1968, 2.8 million; and in 1971, it rose to 5 million. In England, the unemployment situation was also very serious. The number of unemployed workers in 1952 was 500,000. By February 1972, it had increased to more than 1.6 million.

Second, the decline of real wages. The lot of the employed workers in a capitalist country is not any better. The wage of the worker is often below the value of labor power, so that it is difficult for the worker to maintain normal livelihood. Sometimes through struggles with the capitalist, the nominal wage may be increased a little. But since widespread inflation exists in the capitalist countries, the increase in the money wage is often behind the increase in prices. In the end, not only is the real wage not increased, it may even decline. For example, according to official United States statistics, from December 1969 to December 1970 the wages of manufacturing workers increased by 2.6 percent. In the same period, the consumer price index rose by 5.5 percent. Therefore, the real wage of the manufacturing workers declined by 2.9 percent. Besides, there are numerous taxes in the capitalist countries which take away a substantial portion of the income of the laboring people. According to official United States statistics: In the thirty years between 1940 and 1970, the amount of taxation increased by sixteen times. The total private debt of the United States (including housing mortgages and consumer credit) was 197.8 billion dollars, averaging $1,133 per capita. At the end of 1970, the total private debt rose to 577.9 billion dollars, averaging $2,832 per capita. In 1970, repayment of debts and payment of interest of the American people amounted to an average of 22.3 percent of their annual incomes. Taxation, repayment of debts, and payment of interest amounted to about half of the annual income of the American people.

Third, poor living conditions. Because of low real wages, the worker in a capitalist country must put up with poor living conditions. Poor living conditions are especially pronounced with respect to housing conditions. Due to the anarchic conditions of production in capitalist society and the blind concentration of industrial production and population, the size of a few cities gets larger and larger, and the housing conditions of the worker steadily deteriorate. Marx pointed out, 'The faster the capital accumulation of an industrial city or a commercial city, the faster the inflow of human material available for exploitation, and the worse the temporary accommodations arranged for them." (9) Marx and Engels commented several times in their works on the deterioration of the worker's housing conditions under capitalism and described the extremely poor conditions of the slum areas in big cities such as London. Today,the number of slums in the big cities of the capitalist countries is still increasing. In New York City, the biggest American city, the number of people living in slum areas was 1.664 million in 1950. By 1957, it had increased to 2.572 million. The total population of the United States in 1959 was about 180 million, of which 22 million lived in urban slums with 44 million people living in substandard dwellings.

Pollution hazards such as exhaust fumes, waste materials, and effluents further degrade the worker's housing conditions and adversely affect his health. The more developed industry is, the more serious the urban pollution is. The rich capitalists can live in their garden villas in the suburbs and leave the working masses behind to suffer. In some big cities of the capitalist countries which have serious air pollution, each inhabitant inhales a large amount of poisonous gases. In these cities, the incidence of emphysema, bronchitis, and asthma is very high, and the resulting casualty rate is correspondingly high. In Europe, the United States, and Japan, the number of workers who are dismissed because of emphysema is increasing.

In the United States, as far as medical care conditions are

concerned, "the front doors of the hospital are wide open, but there is no entry for the sick who cannot afford to pay." The registration fee for one visit amounts to one-third of the daily wage of a worker with medium income. The operating fee for appendicitis amounts to more than two months' wages. An ordinary worker's family must save for several months before they can afford the delivery fee. From 1965 to 1972, the annual increase in hospitalization fees was 12.3 percent on the average. The consulting fee increased by an annual average of 6.1 percent. Many workers go to work even when they are ill because they cannot afford to pay the consulting fee, and they die prematurely as a result.

Fourth, excessive labor intensity and poor laboring conditions. With the development of mechanization and automation in enterprises, not only are workers increasingly converted into appendages of machines, but labor intensity is also greatly increased. One American auto worker complained: "In ancient Greece and the Roman Empire, even the unfortunate sailor could rest beside his oar for awhile when the wind was favorable. Now, the worker working beside a conveyer belt cannot even take a breath when the machine parts come rolling one after another." As a result of the adoption of the "acceleration system" to intensify exploitation and oppression of the worker, some workers in American plants lose their labor capacity after working for eight to ten years. Many more workers cannot adjust to fast work when they reach forty years old. Because of the fast working pace and the lack of labor protection facilities, accidents at work are numerous. The United States government has to admit that at least 85 percent of American workers work under the constant risk of injury. Every year 3 to 5 percent of American workers die or are injured in industrial accidents. Thus, the advancements in science and technology in the capitalist countries are achieved at the expense of the working class's steady impoverishment and misery.

It is irrefutable, as demonstrated by the above-mentioned facts, that impoverishment does exist in capitalist society.

The bourgeoisie and their agents hidden in the ranks of the proletariat attempt in vain to deny the existence of the proletariat's impoverishment by pointing to the phenomena of some temporary, local, and partial improvements.

First, we must analyze the question of the impoverishment of the proletariat from the class viewpoint. We must first eliminate those worker-aristocrats in the ranks of the proletariat who have been bought by the bourgeoisie. A handful of worker-aristocrats has indeed enjoyed a higher standard of living at the charity of the bourgeoisie. They are no longer members of the workers' ranks, but renegades of the proletariat.

On the issue of the impoverishment of the proletariat, we must analyze it from an historical and concrete viewpoint. Since the standards of living at different times and in different countries are not the same, it is impermissible to make a simple comparison of the present with the past. In the past, even an emperor could only use oil lamps. Today, most workers in the capitalist countries use electric lights. One cannot say that since the workers have electric lights there is no poverty. Would it not be absurd to claim that the life of a worker today is better than that of an emperor?

On the issue of the impoverishment of the proletariat, we must take an overall viewpoint. The so-called overall viewpoint means that we should not judge the living conditions of the workers on the basis of an individual plant, a special locality, or a specific period. We should judge the living conditions of the working class over a long period of time. In other words, we must look at not only the living conditions of the employed workers, but also at the living conditions of the unemployed and semi-unemployed workers. We must look at not only the living conditions of the working class in the imperialist countries, but also at the living conditions of the working class in the colonies.

We must look at not only the living conditions of the working class in times of illusory capitalist prosperity, but also at the working conditions of the working class in times of economic crisis. Then, it is not difficult to tell that while the living conditions of the workers might have improved in individual plants and localities and at some particular times, the conditions of the whole working class are steadily becoming poorer.

The Proletariat Is the Gravedigger of Capitalism

The process of capital accumulation is the process by which the bourgeoisie gets richer and the proletariat gets poorer. It is also a process in which the contradictions between the production relations and productive forces of capitalism are increasingly more acute. In the development process of the capitalist economy, scattered, isolated, and small-scale individual production is transformed into large-scale social production. The development of social production under capitalism consists of two aspects: First, the capitalist plant is different from the small workshop of the individual handicraftsman. In the handicraft workshop, the handicraftsman single-handedly completes the production process. In the capitalist plant, tens, hundreds, or thousands of workers are distributed in various workshops and sections. They complete the manufacture of commodities through division of labor and cooperation under the orders of the capitalist and his agents. Second, social division of labor steadily develops. Production becomes more specialized. The various departments and enterprises in social production are closely associated and dependent on one another. With the development of intraplant and social division of labor, production is "transformed from a series of individual actions into a series of social actions. Products are transformed from individual products into social products." (10) Lathes, automobiles, cotton fabrics, and leather shoes are products of the joint labor of many workers. Nobody can say, 'This is my product." Production becomes social in nature. But the means of production and the products from social labor do not belong to society. They belong to the capitalist himself. Thus, contradictions between social production and capitalist private ownership arise. This is the basic contradiction of capitalism. Capitalist private ownership severely restricts- the development of large-scale social production. Capitalist production relations increasingly restrict the development of productive forces and become fetters to the development of productive forces. Only by demolishing private ownership and establishing socialist collective ownership and by substituting socialist production relations for capitalist relations can this basic contradiction be resolved. Therefore, the extinction of capitalism and the emergence of socialism is an inevitable trend of historical development that cannot be changed by man's will.

But the historical process in which socialism replaces capitalism cannot be spontaneously realized. The bourgeoisie, which benefits from the capitalist system, will inevitably obstruct the social transformation. To realize this transformation, there must be a social force that crushes the resistance of the bourgeoisie. This social force is the proletariat. The proletariat is the representative of advanced productive forces. It is oppressed and exploited, but it is the most conscious class with the most thoroughly revolutionary nature. Under the education of Marxism, it will surely rise to overthrow the capitalist system. "The contradiction between social production and capitalist possession is expressed as the opposition between the proletariat and the bourgeoisie." (11) The proletariat matures and grows steadily in the process of capital accumulation.

The process of capital accumulation and expanded reproduction is not only the expanded reproduction of material means of livelihood, but also the expanded reproduction of capitalist production relations. It produces bigger capitalists on the one hand and more hired laborers on the other. Therefore, the process of capital accumulation not only prepares the material conditions for the extinction of capitalism, namely large-scale production on a social basis, but also produces the gravedigger of capitalism — the proletariat. 'The bourgeoisie not only has forged weapons for its own destruction, it has also trained people who will use these weapons — modern workers, namely the proletariat." (12) The proletariat emerged with the appearance of capitalism and strengthened and became conscious in the process of capital accumulation. With the development of capital accumulation, the ranks of the proletariat gradually swell; with large-scale social production, organizational discipline is instilled in the proletariat; and with the impoverishment of the proletariat, the contradictions between the proletariat and the bourgeoisie steadily deepen. Experienced in clast struggle and armed with Marxism, the proletariat becomes a forward-looking, selfless class richly endowed with revolutionary thoroughness.

In the process of capital accumulation, the great development of social production inevitably reaches a stage when it can no longer be accommodated in the capitalist bombshell. Marx confidently announced: "This bombshell will explode. The knell of capitalist private ownership is about to toll. The expropriator will be expropriated." (13) Capitalism will surely pass away, and socialism will triumph. This is an historical tendency of capital accumulation.

Major Study References

Marx, Capital, Vol. 1, Part 7.

Marx, "The Impoverishment of the Capitalist Society." Chairman Mao, "The Bankruptcy of the Idealist Conception of History."

Review Problems

1. What conclusions can we reach by the analysis of simple reproduction and expanded reproduction?

2. What are the reasons for worker unemployment and the impoverishment of the proletariat in capitalist society?

3. Why do we say that the proletariat is the gravedigger of capitalism?

Notes

1) Marx, Capital, Vol. 1, Complete Works of Marx and Engels, Vol. 23, p. 625.

2) Ibid., p. 649.

3) Ibid., pp. 649-650.

4) Ibid., p.672.

5) Ibid., p. 692.

6) "The Bankruptcy of the Idealist Conception of History," Selected Works of Mao Tse-tung, Vol. 4, Jen-min ch'u-pan- she, 1968, pp. 1400-1401.

7) Marx, Capital, Vol. 1, Complete Works of Marx and Engels, Vol. 23, p. 707.

8) "The Impoverishment of the Capitalist Society," Complete Works of Lenin, Vol. 18, p. 430.

9) Marx, Capital, Vol. 1, Complete Works of Marx and Engels, Vol. 23, p. 725.

10) Engels, Anti-Duhring, Selected Works of Marx and Engels, Vol. 3, Jen-min ch'u-pan-she, 1972, p. 309.

11) Ibid., p. 311.

12) Communist Manifesto, Selected Works of Marx and Engels, Vol. 1, Jen-min ch'u-pan-she, 1972, p. 257.

13) Marx, Capital, Vol. 1, Complete Works of Marx and Engels, Vol. 23, pp. 831-832.

6. The Process of the Movement of Capital Is the Process of Exploiting and Realizing Surplus Value

The Circular Flow of Capital, the Turnover of Capital, and the Reproduction of Social Capital

Capital must be in constant motion to play its role. It passes from the exchange process to the production process and then from the production process to the exchange process in an endless repetition.

In the previous two chapters, we temporarily ignored the exchange process and looked at capital in the production process. In this chapter, we shall analyze the motion of capital and its inherent contradictions from the exchange viewpoint.

The Circulation of Capital Passes through Three Phases and Takes Three Forms

The Three Phases of Capital Circulation Represent the Unity between the Production Process and the Exchange Process

In its motion, capital passes successively through three phases and takes three corresponding forms.

In the first phase of capital motion, the capitalist must first take out a certain amount of money to purchase means of production and labor force in the market. Using G to represent money, W commodities, A labor force, and Pm means of production, this process can be illustrated as follows:

$$G - W \left\langle {A \atop Pm} \right.$$

In this phase, the money in the capitalist's hands serves as a means of purchase and a means of payment. However, at the same time, it also serves as capital because what the capitalist purchases are the labor force and means of production needed to extract surplus labor from the laborer. Here money becomes money capital. Through the purchase of means of production and labor power, money capital is transformed into production capital. Without money capital, there is no production capital and no production of surplus value. The function of money capital is to prepare for the creation of surplus value.

In the second phase of capital motion, the capitalist engages in production by combining the means of production with the labor force. Thus, the exchange process of capital is terminated, and its production process is started. Through this process, labor power is consumed, raw materials are processed, equipment is worn down, and a certain amount of commodities is produced. Production capital is thereby transformed into commodity capital.

The commodity capital in this phase already embodies the surplus value created by the worker. It not only looks different from the commodities bought earlier but also has higher value than the original capital.

This process can be illustrated as follows:

$$W \Big\langle {\genfrac{}{}{0pt}{}{A}{Pm}} \ ...P...W'$$

Here P represents production capital in the production process. The dotted lines before and after P denote the termination of exchange and the beginning of production. W' represents commodities with embodied surplus value.

In this phase, the means of production and the labor force not only play the role of factors of production but also the role of capital because these means of production and labor force are combined in the hands of the capitalist for the production of surplus value. The function of production capital is the production of surplus value.

In the third phase of capital motion, the capitalist must take the commodities which have thus been produced and embodied with surplus value to the market for sale. Through the sale of commodities, commodity capital is again transformed into money capital. Thus, capital is converted back to the form of money.

This process can be illustrated as follows:

$$W'—G'$$

Here G' denotes money capital whose value has been augmented. It consists of both the value of capital advanced by the capitalist and of the realized surplus value. Therefore W'—G' is not only a transformation process in form between commodities and money, but more importantly, is also a process in which the surplus value embodied in the commodities and expropriated by the capitalist is realized. The function of commodity capital is to realize surplus value.

The three phases and three forms of capital show that capital in each of the phases and forms performs an independent function. After a certain function has been performed, it passes into another phase and takes another form. This capital which goes through these successive transformations is industrial capital.

This so-called industrial capital not only includes manufacturing capital, but also the capital in other material production sectors such as agriculture and construction. This capital changes its form successively and passes through three phases to increase its value and then returns to its starting point. This motion is the circulation of capital. Its entire process can be shown as follows:

$$G—W\begin{smallmatrix} A \\ \\ Pm \end{smallmatrix}...P...W'—G'$$

In the circulation of industrial capital, the first and third phases are exchange processes; the second is a production process. The production process plays the determining role in these three phases because it is the only process which can produce surplus value. In the first and third phases, merely the form of capital is transformed; its value remains constant. However, the exchange processes are indispensable for the circulation of industrial capital. Without the exchange processes, the capitalist would not be able to produce and realize surplus value. Therefore, the circular flow of industrial capital is the unity between the production and exchange processes. Because of this, the three phases of circulation in industrial capital must be interrelated, and capital must pass from one phase to another. If the circulation of capital is hindered in the first phase (G—W), it becomes hoarded money and cannot play the role of capital. If its circulation is hindered in the second phase, there will be no production of surplus value. If its circulation is hindered in the third phase, then the surplus value created cannot be realized.

The circulation of Industrial Capital Represents the Unity among Three Circular Flows

To extract surplus value continuously, the capitalist must ensure the continuous circulation of capital. Thus, the formula for the circulation of industrial capital is endless:

$$G—W...P...W'—G'. \quad G—W...P...W'—G'. \quad G—W...P...etc.$$

(1) (2) (3)

The above formula shows that the continuous motion of industrial capital assumes not merely one, but three, circular flows, namely, (1) circulation of money capital: G...G'; (2) circulation of production capital: P...P; and (3) circulation of commodity capital: W'—W'. To ensure the continuous circulation of capital, the capitalist must ensure that his capital exists simultaneously in three forms and that the capital in its three forms circulates continuously according to the circulation flows. For example, say a capitalist has 60,000 yuan of capital. He divides it into three parts, with 20,000 yuan in the form of money capital, 20,000 yuan in the form of production capital, and 20,000 yuan in the form of commodity capital. They are made to circulate along their respective courses. Thus, while this capitalist transforms 20,000 yuan of commodity capital into money capital, 20,000 yuan of production capital is being transformed into commodity capital and 20,000 yuan of commodity capital into production capital. If all 60,000 yuan were in one form, production could not be carried on continuously, but only intermittently. If the circulation of capital in any one of the three forms is hindered in its motion so that circulation is interrupted, for example, if commodities cannot be sold and commodity capital cannot be transformed into money capital, then the circulation of the whole capital is destroyed, and the motion of capital interrupted. Thus, the capitalist is forced to close down production.

The Turnover of Capital Is the Continual Production and Realization of Surplus Value

The Length of Production and Exchange Time Determines the Speed of Capital Turnover

The circulation of capital continues in an endless repetition. The continuous circulation of capital is called the turnover of capital. Marx pointed out,,r When the circulation of capital is regarded as a periodic process and not as isolated incidents, it is called the turnover of capital." (1)

The turnover of capital passes through the production and exchange spheres. The period when capital is in the production sphere is called the production time of capital. The period when capital is in the exchange sphere is called the exchange time of capital. The sum of these two constitutes the turnover period of capital.

The production period of capital includes the following three parts:

First, the period when the means of production perform their function in production. This is primarily the labor time spent by the laborer on objects of labor to produce certain products. The length of labor time is determined by two factors. One is the nature of the production sector. For example, a yarn mill can spin a certain amount of cotton into yarn in one day; but a shipyard takes several months or years to build a ship. Thus, the latter requires longer labor time than the former. Another is the labor productivity of the enterprise. Among enterprises producing the same kind of product, the enterprise with higher labor productivity takes a shorter time to produce the product. On the other hand, a longer time is required by enterprises with lower labor productivity. In some production sectors, the period when the means of production perform their function in the production process also includes time needed for natural forces to act on the objects of labor as well as labor time. For example, wine brewing requires time for fermentation, timber takes time to dry, and crops take time to grow.

Second, the period when production is interrupted but the means of production still stay at the production sites. For example, when machines and equipment are idle at night or because they are out of order.

Third, the period when the means of production have already passed into the production sphere but not into the production process. For example, the time when raw materials are stored.

Among these periods, labor time is the most important. Only in this period can the worker create value and surplus value. Therefore, the capitalist always tries his best to shorten the other times in order to make production time approximate labor tir.ie and extract more surplus value from a given amount of capital in a given period of time.

The exchange period of capital includes both the time for the transformation of money capital into production capital, that is, the time when the capitalist purchases the means of production and labor force, and the time for the transformation of commodity capital into money capital, that is, the time when the capitalist sells his commodities.

The length of capital circulation is determined primarily by the supply and demand conditions in the market, the distance between the point of production and the market, and the conditions of transportation.

Because of the varying effects of the above factors on different production sectors and enterprises, the production period and exchange period of capital vary among them so that the turnover period of capital is not uniform.

Because of the differences in the turnover time of capital, the speed of turnover also varies (the speed of capital turnover is calculated on an annual basis). Suppose the capital of a certain capitalist takes one month to be transformed from money to production capital and from commodity to money capital and the capital production period is three months. Then it takes four months for the capital to turn over once. Thus, the capital turns over three times a year. Further suppose that the capital of another capitalist turns over once every half a year. Then the annual rate of capital turnover is two.

From the above analysis, one knows that the rate of capital turnover is determined ultimately by the production and circulation periods of capital.

The Effects of Capital Composition on the Rate of Capital Turnover

In the above analysis, we assume that every part of the production capital is transformed into commodity capital in one process. But, in fact, the nature and mode of circulation of the various parts of the means of production are all different. From this viewpoint, the composition of production capital can be divided into fixed and working capital.

Fixed capital refers to capital in the form of plants, machines, and equipment. It is paid for in one installment. Its material forms participate in the production process in its entirety and are used more than once. But its value is transferred to the new products gradually according to the rate of depreciation. Because of the special way in which the value of this capital is transferred, we call it fixed capital. For example, if one lathe costs 4,000 yuan and lasts for ten years, then every year 400 yuan of capital value is transferred to the products produced. When the products are sold, 400 yuan of capital value returns to the hands of the capitalist in the form of annual depreciation. The value of this lathe will be completely transferred in ten years.

Working capital refers to that part of the capital which exists in the form of raw materials, fuel, and auxiliary materials or which is used to purchase labor power. Raw materials, fuel, and auxiliary materials lose their material forms in one production process, and their values are completely transferred to the new products in one process. When the products are sold, the total value of this capital returns to the hands of the capitalist in the form of money. Therefore, capital used to buy raw materials, fuel, and auxiliary materials is called working capital. That part of the working capital which is used to purchase labor power does not have its value transferred to the new products. An equivalent value in the new products is created by the new labor of the worker. Although this part of the working capital used to purchase labor power has this characteristic, its mode of value circulation is similar to the working capital used to purchase raw materials, fuel, and auxiliary materials. Because the value produced by the worker in the production process which is equivalent to the value of labor power is also transferred to the products in one process and returns with the sale of products, the capital used to purchase labor power is also working capital.

Now, we know that Marx classified capital into two categories.

In the chapter on the production of surplus value, we talked about the classification of capital into constant and variable capital based on the different roles capital plays in the production of surplus value. This classification makes us understand that surplus value is produced by variable capital and reveals the secret of the capitalist's exploitation of the worker. In this chapter, the classification of capital into fixed and working capital is based on the nature and mode of turnover of various parts of capital. This classification allows us to understand the various factors affecting the speed of capital turnover from the composition of capital.

These two classifications of capital can be illustrated as follows:

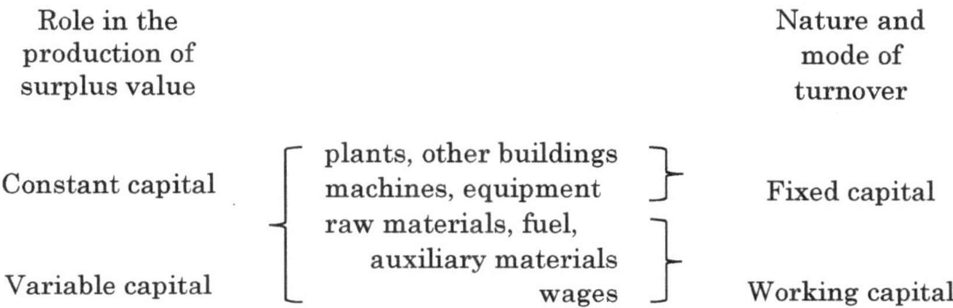

We mentioned above that the value of fixed capital is transferred gradually to new products according to its rate of depreciation. This depreciation has direct effects on the size of the value of fixed capital being transferred and the speed of turnover. To further study the characteristics of fixed capital turnover, we must also analyze the depreciation of fixed capital.

The depreciation of fixed capital can be classified as visible or invisible according to the reasons for its occurrence. Visible depreciation is primarily the result of use in the production process and secondarily of the action of natural forces, such as the decay of timber and the corrosion of iron. Therefore, this depreciation is also called material depreciation. Invisible depreciation is due to the improvement in productipn techniques which reduces the socially necessary labor time to produce similar machines and thus reduces the value of the original fixed capital. It is also due to the appearance of new and better machines, leading to a decrease in the value of the original machines. The depreciation due to a decrease in the value of the original machines is called nonmaterial, or invisible, depreciation. To avoid such depreciation, the capitalist endeavors to lengthen working hours, raise labor intensity, and adopt shifts to accelerate the turnover of capital and increase the exploitation of the worker in order to recover the value of fixed capital as soon as possible.

Because of the differences in the speed of turnover between fixed and working capital, the speed of capital turnover generally refers to the average speed of capital turnover. The general turnover speed of capital advanced is determined by the average turnover speed of various components of capital. The formula to calculate it is to divide the total capital advanced into the total capital turnover in one year. The following table shows the general turnover of capital advanced. All figures are hypothetical.

Components of production capital	Value (yuan)	Number of turnovers per year	Total amount of turnover per year (yuan)
Fixed capital	100,000	1/10	10,000
Plants	30,000	1/30	1,000
Machines	60,000	1/10	6,000
Small tools	10,000	3/10	3,000
Working capital	50,000	4	200,000
Total capital advanced	150,000	1.4	210,000

From the above table, we can see that dividing the total capital advanced, 150,000 yuan, into the total capital turnover, 210,000 yuan, gives us the turnover speed of the total capital advanced as being equal to 1.4. We can also see that the composition of production capital has an effect on the speed of capital turnover. The turnover speed of fixed capital is low, while that of working capital is high. If the share of fixed capital is large, the turnover speed of the total capital will be low. On the other hand, if the share of working capital is large, then the turnover speed of the total capital is high.

The Capitalist Tries His Best to Accelerate the Speed of Capital Turnover to Extract More Surplus Value

The speed of capital turnover has a direct bearing on the production of surplus value. The acceleration of the speed of capital turnover not only can reduce the amount of capital advanced, but can also accelerate the turnover of variable capital in working capital so that more surplus value is produced. Suppose two capitalists both have 2,000 yuan of variable capital and the rate of surplus value is 100 percent for both of them. If the capital of A turns over once a month and the capital of B turns over once every six months, A can obtain 24,000 yuan of surplus value a year, but B can only obtain 4,000 yuan of surplus value a year. Even though their rates of surplus value are equal, the annual rates of surplus value (the ratio between the surplus value produced in one year and the total value of variable capital advanced in one year) are different:

Capitalist A's annual rate

$$\text{of surplus value} = \frac{m}{v} = \frac{24,000}{2,000} = 1,200\%$$

Capitalist B's annual rate

$$\text{of surplus value} = \frac{m}{v} = \frac{4,000}{2,000} = 200\%$$

Therefore, though the amount of variable capital advanced by capitalist A and capitalist B is the same, the speed of capital turnover for capitalist A is six times the speed of capital turnover for capitalist B. Consequently, the surplus value obtained is also six times as great.

The capitalist always tries his best to shorten the turnover time of capital, namely, the production time and exchange time, to accelerate the turnover of capital and obtain more surplus value. To achieve this objective, the capitalist lengthens the worker's labor time, raises labor intensity, and improves production methods in the production sphere to shorten production time. In the exchange sphere, he develops transportation, postal and telecommunications services, and improves business organization to shorten exchange time. However, the inherent contradictions of capitalism hinder the improvement of techniques and impose difficulties on the sale of commodities. Therefore, the capitalist's attempt to accelerate the turnover of capital is not always successful.

Capitalist Reproduction Is Realized Spontaneously amidst Antagonistic Contradictions

Social Capital Is the Sum of Individual Capital

There exist numerous capitalist enterprises in the capitalist society. Each enterprise's individual capital functions independently with respect to other capital to augment value. However, this individual capital is not mutually exclusive. It is interrelated and interdependent because every individual capital must be associated with other capital through the exchange process in order to augment value. Take the example of a yarn mill. It has to be associated with enterprises that supply spinning machines and cotton. On the other hand, it must also be associated with enterprises that consume its products, such as the weaving enterprises. Therefore, close and mutually dependent associations exist between various enterprises. Through these associations, the individual capital forms an organic whole. The sum of this associating individual capital constitutes the social capital. The sum of the movement of the individual capital constitutes the movement of social capital.

Our earlier analysis of the circulation and turnover of capital was conducted from the viewpoint of the reproduction of individual capital. It dealt primarily with the production and realization of surplus value. We have not analyzed where the capitalist sells his commodities, where he purchases his means of production, and where the capitalist and the worker purchase their means of subsistence. However, when we analyze the reproduction of social capital, things are different. Because the social capital already comprises all individual capital, material means consumed in its reproduction process can only be replenished from the total social product. Thus, whether the gross social product can replenish in kind the various inputs consumed in the current production, and if so, how, constitutes an important problem concerning how social reproduction proceeds. As Lenin pointed out: 'The problem now involves where do the worker and the capitalist obtain their consumer goods, where does the capitalist obtain his means of production, and how can products satisfy these needs and permit expanded reproduction? Here it is not only a question of Value replenishment, but also the replenishment of products in kind." (2) Therefore, the reproduction of social capital must be examined in terms of replenishment in value as well asinterms of replenishment in kind.

Marx clearly pointed out that the total social product of capitalism can be divided, in value terms, into constant capital (c), variable capital (v), and surplus value (m). In material terms, it can be classified according to its function in the reproduction process into means of production and means of consumption.

To correspond to the classification of products in kind, Marx divided the whole social product into two sectors: the first was the production of means of production (I), namely, the production of machines, equipment and raw materials; the second was the production of means of consumption (II), namely, the production of food, clothing and daily commodities. Within each category, many production departments were included.

Necessary Conditions for Simple Reproduction

To facilitate exposition, we assume that there are only the bourgeoisie and the proletariat in the capitalist society. The production cycle is one year, and the total value of constant capital is transferred to new products in one production cycle. All commodities are sold according to their values, and there is no fluctuation in the values and prices of commodities; nor is there foreign trade. Under these assumptions, the realization of total social product under simple reproduction can be expressed as follows:

$$\text{I.} \quad 4{,}000\ c + 1{,}000\ v + 1{,}000\ m = 6{,}000$$
$$\text{II.} \quad 2{,}000\ c + 500\ v + 500\ m = 3{,}000$$

Here we assume that in the first sector the constant capital is 4,000, the variable capital 1,000, and the surplus value 1,000. The total value of products is 6,000. Its material forms are the means of production. In the second sector, the constant capital is 2,000, the variable capital

500, and the surplus value 500. The total value of products is 3,000. Its materials are means of consumption.

To continue reproduction, the products of both sectors must be realized. What is the realization of products? It is to say that things that have been consumed must be replenished in value terms and at the same time be replaced in kind. In common language, it must be possible to sell them and buy them back. In the following we will see how the products of these two sectors are realized.

First are the internal exchanges within the first sector. In the beginning of the year when the production process starts in the first sector, there are means of production valued at 4,000. Suppose at the end of the year when the production process is completed, all of them have been consumed. In order to carry on simple reproduction in the second year, new means of production valued at 4,000 must be replenished. Where can the capitalist obtain these means of production? They can only be obtained by exchanging commodities within the sector because only the first category produces means of production. For example, the capitalist of the machine-building plant buys iron and steel from the capitalist of the iron and steel mill, the capitalist of the iron and steel mill buys coking coal from the capitalist of the coking plant and machines from the machine- building plant.... Thus, through exchanges within the first sector, 4,000 c can be replenished and exchanged both in value terms and in material forms. Just as Marx said, "These exchanges are between one type of constant capital and another; that is, between one type of means of production and another.'/ (3)

Next are the internal exchanges within the second sector. In the second sector, when the production process is completed at the end of the year, the worker receives 500 in wages to be spent on personal consumption. The capitalist gets 500 in surplus value. Under simple reproduction, there is no capital accumulation. The 500 in surplus value is also spent on means of consumption. Then, where can they buy the means of production they want? Only within the second sector because only the second sector produces means of consumption. Through internal exchanges within the second sector, that part of the product representing 500 v and 500 m can be realized in value terms as well as in material forms.

Finally, there are exchanges between the two sectors. After the above two types of exchanges, products valued at 1,000 v and 1,000 m still remain in the first sector. In the second sector, products valued at 2,000 c still remain in the second sector. These two remaining parts of products cannot be realized within their own sectors because the 1,000 v and 1,000 m in the first sector, in value terms, should be used for personal consumption by the worker and capitalist. However, these products are means of consumption, not means of production. In the second sector, the 2,000 c in value terms should be used by the capitalist to replenish means of production consumed; but these are means of consumption, not means of production. How can these contradictions be resolved? They can only be resolved through exchanges between the two sectors. The result of these exchanges is that the worker and the capitalist in the first sector obtain their means of consumption and the capitalist of the second sector obtains means of production needed for reproduction the next year. The exchanges between these two sectors can be illustrated in the following chart:

$$\text{I.} \quad 4{,}000 \text{ c} + \boxed{1{,}000 \text{ v} + 1{,}000 \text{ m}} = 6{,}000$$

$$\text{II.} \quad \boxed{2{,}000 \text{ c}} + \quad 500 \text{ v} + \quad 500 \text{ m} = 3{,}000$$

The result of the whole exchange process shows that under simple capitalist production there must be a given proportional relationship between the two sectors; namely, the sum of variable capital and surplus value of the first sector must be equal to the constant capital of the second sector in value terms. In other words, I (1,000 v + 1,000 m) must be equal to II 2,000 c in the above example. Only by maintaining such a proportional relationship can simple capitalist reproduction be carried on. Therefore, I (v + m) = II c is the condition for the realization of social product under simple capitalist reproduction.

Necessary Conditions for Expanded Reproduction

We know that the characteristic of capitalist reproduction is expanded reproduction. To carry on expanded reproduction, the capitalist cannot consume all his surplus value. He must continuously convert part of the surplus value into capital to expand the scale of production. To do so, the capitalist must use part of his newly created capital as constant capital to buy machines and raw materials needed for expanded reproduction. The rest is converted into variable capital to hire additional workers. Therefore, to carry on expanded capitalist reproduction, the total annual products of the first sector must have surplus means of production in addition to those needed to replenish what has been consumed in the first and second sectors during the year. This condition can be expressed in terms of an inequality: I (c + v + m) > I c + n c. Both sides of the inequality contain I c, showing that means of production consumed in the first sector can be replenished from within the same sector. If we cancel out internal replenishments and concentrate on the relationship between the first and the second sectors, the above formula can be expressed as I (v + m) > II c. This is to say that the variable capital and surplus value of the first sector should be larger than the constant capital of the second sector. This is a precondition for expanded capitalist reproduction.

The following chart is used to show how the social product is realized under conditions of expanded capitalist reproduction:

    I.   4,000 c + 1,000 v + 1,000 m = 6,000

    II.   1,500 c +   750 v +   750 m = 3,000

The above are hypothetical production figures for the first year. They meet the requirement for I (c + v + m) > I c + II c or I (v + m) > n c. Now that the capitalist wants to expand reproduction, he cannot spend all the extracted surplus value on consumption. Suppose the capitalist in the first sector spends half of 1,000 m on personal consumption and converts the other half as added capital in the same proportion as the original organic composition of capital, that is, 4 :1 (4,000 c : 1,000 v). The distribution of 1,000 m is as follows:

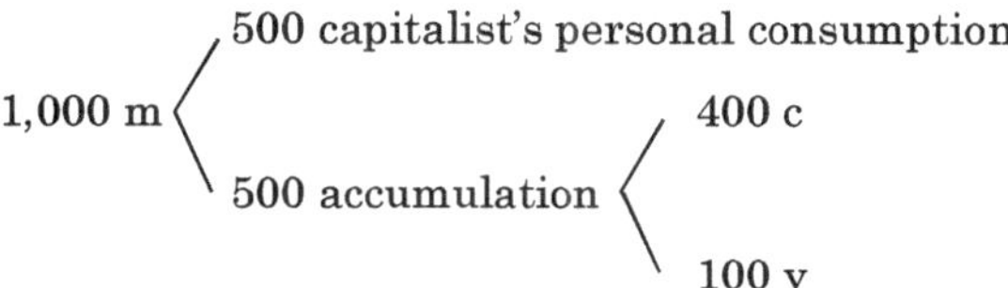

We know that the 400 for added constant capital in the first sector is spent on means of production. Its material forms are also means of production. Therefore, they can be obtained through internal exchanges within the first sector. But the 100 for added variable capital in the first sector is used to hire additional workers who will spend it on means of consumption. However, its material forms are means of production. Therefore, it must be exchanged with the second sector to obtain means of consumption.

Because the material forms of the added variable capital 100 in the first sector are means of production and must be exchanged with the second sector for means of consumption, this creates conditions for expanded reproduction in the second sector. But it also requires the second sector to carry on corresponding capital accumulation for expanded reproduction to meet the increased demand for means of consumption from expanded reproduction in both sectors. Suppose the capitalist of the second sector exchanges part of his surplus value (100 m) for means of production from the first sector to be converted into added constant capital and uses another 50 m as added variable capital in order to conform to the proportion of the original organic composition of capital in the second sector, namely 2 :1 (1,500 c : 750 v). Then 750 m will be distributed as follows:

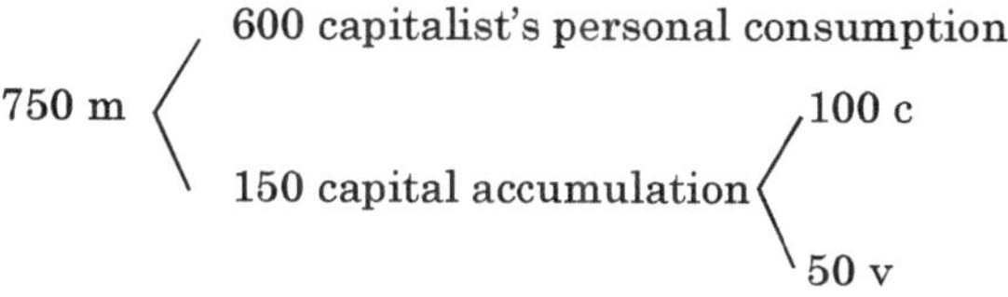

Through the above capital accumulation, the products of the two sectors are rearranged as follows:

$$\text{I.} \quad (4{,}000 \text{ c} + 400 \text{ c}) + (1{,}000 \text{ v} + 100 \text{ v}) + 500 \text{ m} = 6{,}000$$
$$\text{II.} \quad (1{,}500 \text{ c} + 100 \text{ c}) + (750 \text{ v} + 50 \text{ v}) + 600 \text{ m} = 3{,}000$$

Thus, the capital of the two sectors is larger than the original capital advanced, and the conditions for expanded scale of production in the following years in both sectors are guaranteed.

Then, under the condition of expanded reproduction, how are the products of the two sectors realized?

Under the condition of expanded reproduction, the realization of social production is carried on in three aspects just as in simple reproduction: internal exchanges within the first sector, internal exchanges within the second sector, and exchanges between the two sectors. In terms of charts, it is:

$$\text{I.} \quad (4{,}000 \text{ c} + 400 \text{ c}) + \boxed{(1{,}000 \text{ v} + 100 \text{ v}) + 500 \text{ m}} = 6{,}000$$
$$\text{II.} \quad \boxed{(1{,}500 \text{ c} + 100 \text{ c})} + (750 \text{ v} + 50 \text{ v}) + 600 \text{ m} = 3{,}000$$

Through the above exchanges, the capital of each sector is larger than the original capital advanced. The composition of capital in the second year is as follows:

$$\text{I.} \quad 4{,}400 \text{ c} + 1{,}100 \text{ v} = 5{,}500$$
$$\text{II.} \quad 1{,}600 \text{ c} + \phantom{1{,}}800 \text{ v} = 2{,}400$$

If the rate of exploitation stays at 100 percent in this year, the production of the two sectors in the second year is:

$$\text{I.} \quad 4,400 \text{ c} + 1,100 \text{ v} + 1,100 \text{ m} = 6,600$$
$$\text{II.} \quad 1,600 \text{ c} + 800 \text{ v} + 800 \text{ m} = 3,200$$

Compared with the first year, expanded reproduction has been realized.

The Contradictions of Capitalist Reproduction Are Antagonistic

Through the above analysis, we know the necessary conditions for the realization of social product under capitalist simple and expanded reproduction. But this is not to say that these conditions always exist in the capitalist society. In fact, these conditions are frequently violated in the capitalist society. Just as Lenin pointed out: "Abstract theory of realization assumes, and should assume, that products are distributed proportionally in the various departments of capitalist production. But such an assumption does not imply that products are, or can always be, distributed proportionally in the capitalist society." (4) This is due to the fact that in the capitalist society, means of production and products are privately owned by the capitalist and the whole social production is governed by competition and chaotic production conditions. Thus, the proportional relationship between the two sectors and among production departments within each of the sectors is frequently violated. Because of the antagonistic contradiction due to the immense increase of productive forces in the capitalist society and the relative decrease of effective demand from the laboring masses, the necessary proportional relationship between the two sectors cannot always be maintained. Therefore, capitalist reproduction cannot but encounter all sorts of difficulties and obstacles.

There exists a series of antagonistic contradictions in the capitalist reproduction process. These contradictions in due course inevitably lead to economic crises.

Major Study References

Marx, Capital, Vol. 2, chaps. 1, 2, 3, 7, 8, 20, 21.

Lenin, "On the So-called Problem of the Market," Complete Works of Lenin, Vol. 1.

Review Problems

1. How does the capitalist extract more surplus value through the circulation and turnover of capital?
2. What are the conditions for the realization of capitalist reproduction? Are these conditions always satisfied in the capitalist society? Why?

Notes

1) Marx, Capital, Vol. 2, Complete Works of Marx and Engels, Vol. 24, p. 174.
2) "The Development of Russian Capitalism," Complete Works of Lenin, Vol. 3, p. 31.
3) Marx, Capital, Vol. 2, Comple te Works of Marx and Engels, Vol. 24, p. 473.
4) "The Theory of Realization Once Again," Complete Works of Lenin, Vol. 4, p. 61. ~~ '

7. The Entire Bourgeoisie Exploits and Oppresses the Workers

The Division of Surplus Labor

In the capitalist society, the worker is subject to the exploitation and oppression not only of the capitalist of the enterprise to which he belongs, but also of the whole bourgeoisie, consisting of the industrial capitalist, the commercial capitalist, the banking capitalist, and the landed class. Industrial profit, commercial profit, banking profit, interest, and land rent are all extracted from the worker and are all transformed surplus value. Then, how do the various exploiting cliques divide up surplus value? And how is surplus value transformed into profit, interest, land rent, and other concrete forms? These are the problems we will be dealing with in this chapter.

Competition among the Industrial Capitalists Leads to the Equalization of the Rate of Profit

Profit Is Transformed Surplus Value

The insatiable greed for surplus value is the nature of the capitalist. What the capitalist exploits is the surplus value created by the surplus labor of the worker. But in appearance, it is revealed as the capitalist's profit. What then is the distinction and connection between profit and surplus value?

We know that the capitalist must advance some capital in order to exploit the surplus value created by the worker. Of this capital, a part is used to purchase means of production, and the rest is used to purchase labor power for the capitalist production process. In Chapter 4, we stated that that part of the capital used to purchase means of production is constant capital whose value remains unchanged in the production process. That part of the capital used to purchase labor power is variable capital which realizes value augmentation in the production process and brings surplus value to the capitalist. Hence, surplus value is created by the working class and is a product of variable capital. But when the capitalist computes his rate of profit, he compares the surplus value with the total capital advanced as if surplus value is the product of the total capital advanced. Thus, "surplus value, as a conceptual product to recompense total capital, is transformed into profit." (1)

Just as surplus value is transformed into profit, the rate of surplus value is transformed into the rate of profit. The ratio of surplus value to variable capital is the rate of surplus value. Its formula is: surplus value/variable capital, or m/v. The ratio of surplus value to total capital is the rate of profit. Its formula is: surplus value/total capital advanced, or m/c + v.

After surplus value is transformed into profit, the real source of surplus value is concealed, as if constant capital can also bring surplus value to the capitalist. And after the rate of surplus value is transformed into the rate of profit, the degree of exploitation of the worker by the capitalist is concealed. For example, a capitalist advances 10,000 yuan as total capital, of which 8,000 yuan is constant capital and 2,000 yuan is variable capital. Surplus value extracted in one year is 2,000 yuan. The rate of surplus value is 2,000/2,000, or 100 percent. But the rate of profit is 2,000/8,000 + 2,000, or 20 percent, much lower than the rate of surplus value. Therefore, the purpose of the capitalist in treating surplus value as the product of the total capital advanced is to conceal the real source of surplus value and the degree of exploitation of the worker.

Competition among Capitalists of Various Sectors Equalizes Profit

To go after profit is the class nature of the capitalist. The intent of the capitalist is always to obtain the maximum amount of profit by advancing the smallest amount of capital. The capitalists not only cruelly exploit the worker, they also compete fiercely among themselves.

Competition among capitalists is carried on both among enterprises in the same sector and among sectors. In the competition among enterprises in the same sector, those capitalists adopting new techniques are in a favorable position. The labor productivity of their enterprises is high, and the individual labor time is below the socially necessary labor time so that excess surplus value is obtained. This excess surplus value is transformed into excess profit which is pocketed by the capitalist who adopts new techniques. A different result is obtained in competition among sectors. It leads to a uniform rate of profit among them. The capitalists of various sectors divide up the surplus value created by the worker according to the principle of equal profit for equal capital.

Let us now analyze how competition among the capitalists of various sectors leads to a uniform rate of profit.

In the capitalist society, the rate of profit varies among production sectors with their different organic composition of capital. The organic composition of capital is the ratio of constant capital to variable capital, and surplus value is only the result of the augmentation of variable capital. Hence, under the condition of a uniform rate of surplus value, the higher the organic composition of capital is, that is, the larger the share of constant capital and the smaller the share of variable capital, the smaller the surplus value given an equal amount of advanced capital. The rate of profit is also lower. On the other hand, the lower the organic composition of capital, the higher the rate of profit will be. Suppose shoemaking, spinning and weaving, and machine building are the three sectors of society. The organic composition of capital is 7: 3 in the shoemaking sector, 8 :2 in the spinning and weaving sector, and 9:1 in the machine-building sector. The capital of each of these three sectors is 10,000 (in units of thousands of yuan or ten thousands of yuan or any other convenient unit), and the rate of surplus value is 100 percent.

To facilitate analysis, we further assume the rate of capital turnover in these three sectors is once a year. The value of constant capital is completely transformed in one year to products of that year. Thus, with a 100 percent rate of surplus value, the shoemaking sector obtains a profit of 3,000, the spinning and weaving sector obtains a profit of 2,000, and the machine- building sector obtains a profit of 1,000. The organic composition of capital is lowest in the shoemaking sector. Its rate of profit is 30 percent. The organic composition of capital is highest in the machine-building sector. Its rate of profit is the lowest, only 10 percent. The organic composition of capital in the spinning and weaving sector is in the middle with a rate of profit of 20 percent. It is lower than that of the shoemaking sector, but higher than that of the machine-building sector.

Such a condition of equal investment with unequal profit cannot long exist in capitalist society. The capitalist always tries to invest capital in the production sector with the highest rate of profit. Therefore, the above condition must undergo changes. First of all, some capitalists of the machine-building sector will withdraw from production and invest their capital in the shoemaking sector for a higher rate of profit. Such a transfer of capital greatly boosts the output of the shoemaking sector.

As supply gradually exceeds demand, the price comes down. On the other hand, the output of the machine-building sector is gradually reduced. The supply of machines gradually falls short of the demand for them, and the price gradually goes up. A combination of capital transfers and price adjustments leads to a more or less uniform rate of profit. This is then the average rate of profit. It is the result of comparing the total societal surplus value with the total societal capital. If we take the three sectors as representing the total societal production, the total societal surplus value is 6,000, and the total societal capital is 30,000. The average rate of profit is 6,000/30,000 = 20 percent. The profit obtained according to the average rate of profit is called the average profit. Marx pointed out, 'The average profit is merely the amount of surplus value distributed proportionally to each production sector according to its capital share." (2)

The category of average profit reflects the relationship among the capitalists of various sectors in dividing up the surplus value created by the working class of society.

The formation of average profit further conceals the capitalist exploitative relationship. The transformation of surplus value into profit already confuses the source of surplus value. But the profit obtained by the capitalists in various production sectors is still equal to the surplus value created by the workers of the respective sectors.

After the formation of average profit, the capitalists of various sectors divide up surplus value so that the profit obtained by the various sectors is no longer equal to their respective surplus value produced. Now, provided that each sector possesses an equal amount of capital, an equal amount of surplus value can be obtained. The size of profit is entirely determined by the size of the capital advanced. This further obscures the nature of profit and the exploitative relationship it reflects.

The Equalization of the Rate of Profit Transforms the Value of Commodities into Production Price

After the formation of average profit, the capitalist no longer sells commodities according to their values, but according to their production prices. Production price is equal to cost plus average profit. Based on the earlier assumptions, the formation process of production price is shown in the following table.

Production sector	Constant capital (1)	Variable capital (2)	Surplus value (3)	Commodity value (4) = (1) + (2) + (3)	Average profit rate (%) (5)	Average profit (6) = [(1)+(2)] × (5)	Commodity production price (7) = (1) + (2) + (6)	Production price minus value (8) = (7) − (4)
Shoe making	7,000	3,000	3,000	13,000	20	2,000	12,000	-1,000
Spinning and weaving	8,000	2,000	2,000	12,000	20	2,000	12,000	0
Machine building	9,000	1,000	1,000	11,000	20	2,000	12,000	+1,000
Total	24,000	6,000	6,000	36,000	20	6,000	36,000	0

From the table, we can see that in the machine-building sector where the organic composition of capital is high, the production price of the commodity is higher than its value, while in the shoemaking sector where the organic composition of capital is lower, the production price is lower than value. Only in the spinning and weaving sector where the organic composition of capital is in the middle is the production price equal to value.

With the formation of average profit and the transformation of value into production price, market price no longer fluctuates around value, but around production price. Does the appearance of production price mean that the law of value no longer matters? No. From the viewpoint of the individual capitalists in various sectors, some sell their commodities at production prices above value and obtain more profit than the surplus value created by their sector, while others sell their commodities at production prices below value and obtain less profit than the surplus value created by their sector. However, from the viewpoint of the whole society, the total value of commodities is equal to the total production price. The total average profit obtained by the industrial capitalists as a whole is equal to the total surplus value created by the industrial workers as a whole. Therefore, production price is merely a transformation of value.

Marx's theory about average profit tells us: In capitalist so
ciety, the worker is subject to the exploitation and oppression
not only of the capitalist in his own enterprise, but also of the
industrial capitalists as a whole.

The Commercial Capitalists Share in the Surplus Value through Commodity Transactions

The Role of Commercial Capital Is to Realize Surplus Value

In the above analysis, we suppose the surplus value created by the working class was monopolized by the industrial capitalist. In fact, the industrial capitalist cannot monopolize it. He must transfer part of the surplus value extracted from the worker to the commercial capitalist. The commercial capitalist does not engage in commodity production;

he merely advances capital to buy commodities in bulk from the industrial capitalist and sells them to help the industrial capitalist in realizing surplus value. This surplus value obtained by the commercial capitalist is called commercial profit.

Why does the industrial capitalist need the commercial capi- talist to sell commodities for him, and why is he willing to share a part of the surplus value extracted with the commercial capitalist? Because with the development of capitalism, the volume of commodities produced by the industrial capitalist steadily increases, and the market for commodities steadily expands. If the industrial capitalist has to handle the business of commodity sales, he must establish a large commercial organization and hire a large number of shop assistants. This is not profitable for the industrial capitalist because a large amount of capital would have to be tied down to the exchange process, thus adversely affecting his scale of production and competitive power. If the sale of commodities is delegated to the commercial capitalist specializing in commodity transactions, he can benefit from the advantages of specialization in commodity transaction and save on exchange expenses. In addition, because of the existence of the independent activities of commercial capital, the industrial capitalist can sell his commodities to the commercial capitalist in bulk and more quickly complete the transformation from commodity capital to money capital. Consequently, his capital can be active in the production sphere and play the role of productive capital longer for the extraction of more surplus value. Thus, though a part of the surplus value has to be transferred to the commercial capitalist, it is still to the advantage of the industrial capitalist after all. This is why commercial capital is separated from industrial capital.

Commercial Capital Also Participates in the Formation of Average Profit

By helping the industrial capitalist realize surplus value by investing in commerce, the commercial capitalist not only requires commercial profit, he also requires that this commercial profit not be lower than the average profit of industrial capital. Otherwise, the commercial capitalist would rather invest his capital in the production sector than engage in commerce.

Where does commercial profit come from? On the surface, it appears that commercial profit is brought about by the sale of commodities above their value. The bourgeoisie takes advantage of this illusion and says that commercial profit arises from exchange. This is a distortion of the source of commercial profit and a concealment of exploitation.

In fact, commercial profit is also a part of the surplus value extracted from the worker by the industrial capitalist. Because the industrial capitalist wants the commercial capitalist to sell commodities for him, he cannot sell his commodities according to their production price, but must sell below production price. The commercial capitalist then sells the commodities at production price to the consumers. In this way, a part of the surplus value extracted from the worker by the industrial capitalist is transferred to the commercial capitalist.

For example, suppose the industrial capitalist in society invests 40 billion yuan in a year, of which 30 billion yuan is constant capital, 10 billion yuan is variable capital, and 10 billion yuan is surplus value. Suppose the production cycle is one year, and the value of constant capital is completely transferred to products in one year. Then, the total value of commodities, or the total production price, is 30 billion yuan + 10 billion yuan + 10 billion yuan = 50 billion yuan. The rate of profit is 10/40 = 25 percent. But the circulation of commodities must be handled by the commercial capitalist. Suppose the total value of commercial capital is 10 billion yuan. Then the total capital in the production and exchange spheres is 50 billion yuan. The 10 billion yuan of surplus value must be shared equally between the 50 billion yuan of industrial and commercial capital. The average profit rate can no longer be 25 percent, but instead is 20 percent. According to the average profit rate of 20 percent, the industrial capitalist obtains 8 billion yuan, and the commercial capitalist obtains 2 billion yuan. That the commercial capitalist can obtain this 2 billion yuan of profit is because the industrial capitalist sells his commodities to the commercial capitalist at a price below their production price, that is, at the price of 48 billion yuan (40 billion yuan in cost and 8 billion yuan in profit).

And the commercial capitalist sells the commodities according to the production price of 50 billion yuan and obtains a 2 billion yuan profit. Thus, the 10 billion yuan of surplus value created by the worker is shared proportionally according to the capital advanced by the industrial and commercial capitalists respectively.

The Commercial Capitalist Cruelly Exploits the Employee

The commercial employee is just like the industrial worker. He is a hired laborer and subject to the exploitation of the bourgeoisie. The difference between them is that the industrial worker produces surplus value in the production sphere for the capitalist under his supervision, while the commercial employee realizes surplus value for the capitalist in the exchange sphere under his supervision. Why do we say the commercial employee is subject to exploitation just like the industrial worker? This is because the commercial employee and the industrial worker earn their livings by selling labor power. The value of their labor power has to be determined by labor time needed to reproduce labor power. Although the commercial employee does not create value or surplus value through his labor connected with commodity transactions, the value of commodities and the surplus value embodied must be realized through his labor. Therefore, the labor time of the employee is also divided into necessary labor time and surplus labor time. The part of surplus value realized in the necessary labor time through the employee's sale of commodities goes to compensate the variable capital with which the commercial capitalist buys the labor power of the employee. In the surplus labor time, the employee works for the commercial capitalist for free in order to enable the commercial capitalist to share part of the surplus value from the industrial capitalist as commercial profit. Therefore, the commercial employee, like the industrial worker, is exploited.

The exploitation of the employee by the commercial capitalist is equally cruel. To obtain more commercial profit, the commercial capitalist raises labor productivity by lengthening labor time and increasing labor intensity. He also resorts to deducting wages from the employee and other ruthless means to intensify exploitation. Take the example of the capitalists in the old Shanghai Hsieh-ta-hsiang Silk Goods Company. In order to intensify exploitation of the employee, they set down 120 regulations. The employee was required to work sixteen to seventeen hours a day at high labor intensity. There were so many deductions from his wages that they were not sufficient for a minimum level of subsistence. Under the bloodthirsty extractions of the capitalist, the broad masses of employees, like the multitude of industrial workers, sell not only their labor power but also their lives.

The Financial Capitalists Share in Surplus Value through Loans and Borrowings

The Source of Interest Is Surplus Value

In the capitalist society, the financial capitalist, in addition to the industrial and commercial capitalists, also shares in the surplus value.

There are certain objective necessities for the existence of capital loans and borrowings because, in the capitalist reproduction process, the capitalist may be short of capital. For example, when products have not been sold but machines and raw materials have to be bought and wages paid, some money capital has to be borrowed. Sometimes, there may also be idle money capital. For example, before fixed capital is replaced, the capitalist may have some accumulated depreciation charges in money form. After commodities have been sold but before raw materials have been bought and wages paid, there may also be some idle money capital. Under these circumstances, those capitalists who possess money capital can lend the temporarily idle money capital to capitalists in need of money. The capitalists who borrow this money capital will use it to ^produce or sell commodities to extract or realize surplus value. Naturally, the owners of money capital will not lend it to other capitalists without any compensation. They will demand a certain amount of money from the borrowing capitalists as compensation for the loan. The borrowing capitalist must share a part of the surplus value he extracts with the lending capitalist. This part of surplus value is called interest.

Money capital that is lent for interest is known as loan capital. The ratio of interest to loan capital is called the rate of interest. The highest level of the interest rate cannot exceed the average profit rate. If this is not so, the borrowing capitalists will not get any benefit from the loans and will not borrow. The source of interest is surplus value. However, the apologists of the bourgeoisie advance the false theory that "big money breeds little money" and say that "interest comes from money itself" to conceal the nature and source of interest and the capitalists' exploitative relations.

Bank Profit Is Obtained from the Difference between the Borrowing and Lending Interest

In the capitalist society, the borrowing and lending of money is largely done through the bank. By attracting deposits, the bank collects idle capital and funds which the people do not need for a period of time. It then lends the money to the functioning capitalist. The bank pays interest to attract capital and collects interest from loans. The lending interest rate is higher than the deposit interest rate. This difference between the borrowing and lending interest rates, after subtracting the operating expenses of the bank, constitutes bank profit. Like interest, bank profit also comes from the surplus value created by the worker in production. The banking capitalist shares in the surplus value created by the worker by obtaining the interest differential through borrowings and loans.

The purpose of the banking capitalist in advancing capital to operate the bank is to obtain profit. Therefore, bank profit cannot be lower than the average profit obtained by other functional capitalists. If bank profit is below average profit, he will not run the bank but will instead run plants and shops himself.

The Appearance of Stocks Is a Reflection of the Intensification of the Parasitic Nature of Capitalism

With the development of capitalist production, the scale of enterprises expands. The large amount of capital needed to run large enterprises cannot be afforded by individual capitalists. There arises a need for many individual capitalists to form joint- stock corporations. The joint-stock corporation is an enterprise with pooled capital. It is an important means which big capital uses to control medium and small capital and to manipulate capital.

The joint-stock company issues stocks, and those who purchase the stocks become stockholders. Stockholders have a r ight to share part of the enterprise's profit according to the amount of stock owned. Income from stocks is known as dividends.

The capitalist who owns stocks does not have to work. He can loaf all day long and lead an extravagant life on dividends. The stockholder may also speculate in stocks. The stock exchange is full of dishonest competition. The appearance of people who live on interest by clipping interest coupons and speculating in stocks reflects the intensification of the parasitic nature of capitalism.

The Landed Class Reaps without Sowing

Capitalist Monopoly Operation of Land Leads to Differential Rent

Landowners are another exploitative class in the capitalist society. They own land and rent it out to the industrial and agricultural capitalist in order to share in the surplus value. To reveal the nature of capitalist rent, we start from the two forms of capitalist rent, namely, differential rent and absolute rent.

Land is the basic means of production for agricultural production. But unlike other means of production, its quantity is limited. This limited quantity of land includes superior, medium, and inferior land with respect to fertility. In the capitalist society, this limited supply of land leads to the capitalist's monopolistic operation of land.

With capitalist monopoly of land, some agricultural capitalists operate superior and medium land; other agricultural capitalists operate inferior land. Because the produce of the superior and medium land cannot fully satisfy the market demand, the price of produce must rise in response to the shortage of supply vis- a-vis demand. It will continue to rise until the agricultural capitalists who operate the inferior land can obtain an average profit. Marx pointed out, "The production price from the poorest land is always the regulating market price." (3) Thus, those agricultural capitalists who operate the superior and medium land will obtain excess profit. This excess profit constitutes differential rent.

There are two forms of differential rent. One arises from the difference in fertility and location and is known as Differential Rent I. The other arises from successive investments on the same piece of land and is known as Differential Rent II.

Let us first take the example of two pieces of crop land of equal size but different fertility:

Unit: yuan

Type of land	Capital invested (1)	Average profit (2)	Output (chin) (3)	Individual production price		Social production price		Differential Rent I (8)
				Total output (4) = (1) + (2)	Unit output (5) = (4) ÷ (3)	Unit output (6)	Total output (7) = (6) × (3)	
Inferior	200	40	4,000	240	0.060	0.060	240	0
Medium	200	40	5,000	240	0.048	0.060	300	60
Superior	200	40	6,000	240	0.040	0.060	360	120

The capital invested in each of the three pieces of land is 200 yuan. Suppose the capital is completely transferred to products. The cost will be 200 yuan in each case. But labor productivity of the agricultural worker is different on land of different fertility. The agricultural output is 4,000 chin, 5,000 chin, and 6,000 chin respectively. If the average profit is 20 percent, then the production price (cost + average profit) of the total output for each piece of land is 240 yuan. But because the output is different for the different pieces of land, the production price of unit output is different. With inferior land, it is

0.060 yuan. With medium land, it is 0.048 yuan. And with superior land, it is 0.040 yuan. The social production price in the market is determined by the unit production price of inferior land, that is, 0.060 yuan per chin. Thus, the agricultural capitalist who operates inferior land obtains 240 yuan. After deducting 200 yuan of cost, an average profit of 40 yuan remains. There is no excess profit or differential rent. The agriculturalists who operate medium and superior land obtain 300 yuan and 360 yuan respectively. After deducting 200 yuan as cost, they get 60 yuan and 120 yuan respectively as excess profit in addition to 40 yuan of average profit. This excess profit constitutes Differential Rent I.

Let us now take the example of continually investing on the same piece of crop land to explain the emergence of Differential Rent II. For example, the agricultural capitalist who operates inferior land invests successively on the same piece of land. He invests 200 yuan the first time. The output of produce is 4,000 chin, and the average profit is 40 yuan with no excess profit or differential rent. If this capitalist invests another 200 yuan the second time to construct water control facilities, add fertilizers, buy new machines, hire more agricultural workers, and increase labor productivity, he may get 5,000 chin more of produce (that is, he invests 400 yuan in total and obtains 9,000 chin). With an unchanged social production price for produce, the total price of the 5,000 chin obtained from the second investment is 300 yuan. After deducting 200 yuan as cost and 40 yuan as average profit, he still has 60 yuan of excess profit. This 60 yuan is Differential Rent II.

We must point out here that the amount of rent was already determined when the agricultural capitalist signed a contract with the landowner. Therefore, within the current contract, the excess profit obtained from successive investment will accrue to the agricultural capitalist. But when the contract expires and is renegotiated, the landowner may again raise the rent. In the end, this excess profit will be transferred to the landowner in the form of Differential Rent II. Marx pointed out: "Differential rent possesses a certain attribute: the ownership of land merely takes away surplus profit. Under a different condition, this surplus profit may be taken away by the tenant. And within the currency of a contract, it is in fact taken away by the tenant." (4) Therefore, the agricultural capitalist always attempts to have a longer contract. But the landowner tries his best to shorten the duration of a contract. Both sides fight to obtain this excess profit. This contradiction between the agricultural capitalist and the landowner makes the agricultural capitalist plunder the fertility of the land as much as he possibly can before the expiration of a contract.

Monopolistic Private Landownership Leads to Absolute Rent

Inferior land does not provide differential rent. But if the owner of inferior land does not get any rent, he would prefer to let the land remain uncultivated rather than let others use it. In fact, the agricultural capitalist who operates inferior land must also pay rent to the landowner. This rent arising from the monopoly of private landownership is called absolute rent.

If the agricultural capitalist who operates inferior land must also obtain an average profit, where does the rent come from?

In the capitalist society, agricultural technology is always behind manufacturing technology. The organic composition of capital in agriculture is always lower than that of manufacturing. We know that surplus value comes from variable capital. Since the organic composition of capital is lower in agriculture than in manufacturing, an equal amount of capital can bring more surplus value in agriculture than in industry. Suppose the average organic composition of capital in manufacturing is 8: 2 and the rate of surplus value is 100 percent. Then, in every 100 yuan of capital, there is 20 yuan in variable capital bringing about 20 yuan in surplus value. The average rate of profit is 20 percent. The value of commodities and the production price are 120 yuan. And suppose the organic composition of capital in agriculture is 6 :4 and the rate of surplus value is 100 percent. Then for every 100 yuan, there is 40 yuan in variable capital bringing about 40 yuan in surplus value. The value of produce is 140 yuan, and the rate of profit is 40 percent. In the capitalist society, agricultural produce can be sold at its value (140 yuan). But the agricultural capitalist can only obtain an average profit equal to that of the industrial capitalist, namely, 20 yuan. The production price of produce is therefore 120 yuan. Now agricultural produce is sold above its production price. In addition to an average profit of 20 yuan, the agricultural capitalist still has 20 yuan surplus which is the difference between the value of agricultural produce and its production price. This constitutes absolute rent.

Why can agricultural produce be sold above its production price? This is because of the existence of monopolistic private landownership. In manufacturing, the organic composition of capital in various departments is not all the same. It is natural for departments with lower organic composition of capital to produce more surplus value. But as a result of interdepartmental competition and the transfer of capital, all industrial capitalists can obtain only an average profit. So industrial products can be sold only at their production price. But, agricultural production is different from manufacturing production. There is one obstacle in agriculture, namely, monopolistic private ownership, which prevents the unconditional transfer of capital to agriculture. This prevents the surplus value in the agricultural sector from participating in the process of profit equalization. And agricultural produce can be sold at a value higher than its production price.

Therefore, in agriculture, even inferior land can obtain more surplus value from an equal amount of capital. This surplus value is not shared with manufacturing. It remains in agriculture and is converted into absolute rent for the landowner.

Capitalist Rent Is Also a Part of Surplus Value

Although the formation of differential and absolute rent arises from different causes, their substance and source are the same. As a result of capitalist monopolistic operation of land, the price of produce is determined by the production price on inferior land. The agricultural capitalist who operates superior and medium land thus reaps excess profit. This excess profit has no connection with private landownership. Even if there is no private landownership, the agricultural capitalist who operates superior and medium land will still obtain this excess profit. Marx pointed out, private landownership "is not the cause of this surplus profit, but the cause of its transformation into rent." (5) As a result of the existence of private landownership, this excess profit is transformed into differential rent. Also because of the existence of monopolistic private landownership, the price of agricultural produce can be set at a value above its production price. Even the agricultural capitalist who operates inferior land can obtain excess profit which is transformed into absolute rent for the landowner. The source of differential rent and absolute rent is excess profit. This excess profit is created by the agricultural worker, just as is the whole surplus value in agriculture. The agricultural capitalist rents land from the landowner, buys means of production, hires agricultural workers to engage in production, and extracts surplus value from the agricultural workers. From this surplus value, the agricultural capitalist obtains an average profit. The surplus value over and above the average profit is transformed into rent. Therefore, the substance of rent is also surplus value.

However, the landowner and his spokesman, in order to conceal the exploitation of the agricultural worker by the landowner and the agricultural capitalist, seize upon the superficial differences between the output of produce from superior and inferior land to insist that "rent is brought about by land itself." This explanation is entirely groundless. Good and superior land only provide favorable conditions for the increase of labor productivity and a natural basis for the creation of surplus profit. But without the labor of the agricultural worker, even the best land cannot create any value. Marx pointed out, "All rent is surplus value and is all a product of surplus labor." (6) Marx's theory of rent thoroughly exposes the fallacious explanation of the land- owner and his spokesman.

Capitalist rent and feudal rent are a result of private land- ownership, but their respective exploitative relations are different. Feudal rent is the total surplus labor or surplus produce that the feudal landlord obtains from the peasant. Capitalist rent is the surplus value over and above an average profit obtained by the agricultural capitalist from the agricultural worker. Feudal rent manifests the exploitative relation between the feudal landlord and the peasant. Capitalist rent manifests the exploitative relation between the landowner and the agricultural capitalist on the one hand and the agricultural worker on the other.

Through the above analysis, we can see that in the capitalist society the bourgeoisie is divided into different exploitative groups. There are the manufacturing, agricultural, commercial, and banking capitalists. The landowner is another exploitative class in the capitalist society. They are all foxes of the same ilk sharing among themselves the surplus value created by the working class and concertedly exploiting and oppressing the working class. Therefore, in the capitalist society, the bourgeoisie is on top of the working class. The contradiction between the worker and the capitalist is the contradiction between the whole working class and the whole bourgeoisie. This is the basic contradiction of the capitalist society. If the working class wants to liberate itself, it must unite as a class, take up guns to make revolution, overthrow the whole bourgeoisie, and destroy the capitalist exploitative relationship.

Major Study References

Marx, Capital, Vol. 3, chaps. 1, 2, 9, 17, 21, 38. 45.

Chairman Mao, "The Analysis of Chinese Social Classes.
"

Chairman Mao, "The Chinese Revolution and the Chinese Communist Party," chap. 2, sections 2, 4.

Review Problems

1. How do the various exploitative groups in the capitalist society exploit the surplus value created by the working class?

2. What is the significance of Marx's theory on the division of surplus value?

Notes

1) Marx, Capital, Vol. 3, Jen-min ch'u-pan-she, 1966, p. 16.

2) Ibid., p. 180.

3) Ibid., p. 772.

4) Ibid., p. 881.

5) Ibid., p. 759.

6) Ibid., p. 744.

8. The Incurable Disease of Capitalism

Economic Crises

Economic crises are the natural product of capitalist economic development. They are pronounced manifestations of the intensification of various contradictions in capitalist production, exchange, distribution, and reproduction. How do capitalist economic crises arise? What are their effects on capitalist development? We will talk about these problems in this chapter.

Economic Crises Are a Product of the Intensification of the Basic Contradictions in Capitalism

Capitalist Economic Crises Are Crises of Overproduction

Before capitalism (for example, in the long history of China's feudal society), there were also many social, economic, and livelihood crises. Because of the cruel exploitation of the peasant by the landlord class, the ravages of war, and natural calamities such as floods, droughts, insect pests, and hailstorms, agricultural production suffered serious damage, the laboring people lost their homes, and hundreds of thousands died of hunger and plagues. Social, economic, and livelihood crises at those times were characterized by insufficient food grain production. Capitalist economic crises are not characterized by insufficient production, but by overproduction. The most notable features connected with capitalist economic crises are: large quantities of commodities cannot be sold, factories close down, banks fold up, values of stocks fall, unemployment figures rapidly increase, productive forces suffer severe damage, and the whole economy is paralyzed and chaotic.

Capitalist economic crises are crises of overproduction. But the so-called "overproduction" is not an absolute overproduction; it does not mean that things produced by society are more than what the masses can consume. In economic crises, the phenomena described below are widespread. Textile workers receive dismissal notices saying that there is an overproduction of yarns and fabrics without sales outlets so production has to be cut back and workers dismissed. However, the textile workers and their families are inadequately clothed. Those who produce fabrics cannot afford them. Miners receive dismissal notices saying that there is an overproduction of coal necessitating production and employment cutbacks. Yet, the miners and their families have to shiver in the cold for lack of money to buy coal. Therefore, capitalist overproduction is relative overproduction. In other words, social production is excessive only in relation to the purchasing power of the masses. During economic crises, inventories pile up in the warehouses of the capitalist for lack of demand. Commodities may be rotting away or even artificially destroyed. On the other hand, the broad laboring masses are too poor to afford food and clothing and are struggling on the verge of starvation.

The economic crisis of overproduction is a special feature of the capitalist economy. Nevertheless, the possibility of economic crises is latent in the development process of the commodity economy from the beginning. When the commodity producer sells his commodities, he does not always immediately use the money obtained to buy means of production or required daily commodities. However, if he does not buy, then those commodity producers who trade with him cannot sell. Here dislocations between sales and purchases may arise, and the possibility of crises exists. However, when commodity production was carried on by petty commodity producers and based on individual ownership, the purpose of production was to trade for other commodities to maintain production and satisfy personal consumption needs. Therefore, sales were usually followed by purchases. At the same time, the productive forces were low, and the scale of production small. Society's division of labor was not well developed, and production interdependencies were not very close. Even if dislocations between sales and purchases arose, their effects were local and would not lead to economic crises affecting the whole society. Therefore, even though commodity production itself embodies the possibility of crises, the inevitability of crises can only be found in the capitalist economic system itself.

The Source of Economic Crises Lies in the Basic Contradiction of Capitalism

Economic crises in the capitalist society are inevitable. This is determined by the basic contradiction of capitalism. Stalin pointed out: "The source and cause of economic crises of overproduction lie in the capitalist system itself. The source of crisis lies in the contradiction between the social nature of production and the capitalist ownership of products." (1)

Why does the basic contradiction of capitalism inevitably lead to economic crises?

First of all, the basic contradiction of capitalism inevitably manifests itself in a contradiction in which the productive forces greatly increase while the purchasing power of the laboring people relatively decreases. Capitalist large-scale social production is very different from individual handicraft production. Individual production is characterized by simple reproduction.

Even under very favorable market conditions, its growth in production is slow. Capitalist production is production by big machines and is capable of rapid growth. The capitalist tries his best to expand production in search of more profit because the larger the scale of production, the more surplus value he can extract. At the same time, the capitalist must also try to improve his techniques and expand his scale of production in order to avoid being squeezed out by other capitalists. With the expansion of production, the standard of consumption must also be increased so that the increased production of commodities can be sold and social production continued. But under the condition of private ownership of the means of production, the capitalist always tries to reduce wages to the lowest possible level. The development of capitalist production and the adoption of new techniques inevitably keep a large number of workers outside the factory gates and expand the ranks of the unemployed. Capitalist competition inevitably renders a large number of peasants and handicraftsmen bankrupt so that small capital is squeezed out or swallowed by big capital. Thus, on the one hand there is an immense growth of production, and on the other hand there is a relative decrease in the purchasing power of the laboring people. This contradiction makes the economic crises of overproduction inevitable.

The basic contradiction of capitalism also inevitably leads to economic crises because the contradiction inevitably manifests itself in a contradiction in which the production of individual factories is organized while social production is chaotic. As production becomes social, the relationship and interdependency among production sectors and among various enterprises are increasingly close. For example, the cotton required by the textile mill is supplied by the agricultural sector, and spinning and weaving machines by the machine-building industry. Therefore, in a given period of time, there must be a unified plan and arrangement to determine the necessary amount of cotton, cloth, and spinning and weaving machines so that social production can be smoothly carried out. However, capitalist private ownership of the means of production divides the whole society into numerous autonomous capitalist enterprises. From the viewpoint of one enterprise, its workers are all controlled by one capital, and its internal production is organized. But from society's viewpoint, what and how much the various enterprises of different capitalists produce are the private business of individual capitalists. Nobody else can say anything about it. Therefore, the production of the society as a whole is carried on under anarchic conditions. Because social production is uncoordinated, individual capitalists cannot possibly know the actual demand for a certain commodity. Provided that there is profit, capitalists will compete among themselves to expand production. At the same time, capitalist commercial activities may also create false demand that conceals the society's actual purchasing power. Even though production actually exceeds the purchasing power of the masses, as long as the market price continues to go up, commercial capitalists will still order from industrial capitalists, and financial capitalists will still extend credit to industrial and commercial capitalists to facilitate industrial capitalists to expand production, thus creating false prosperity in the market. This false prosperity conceals the existence and development of overproduction. When overproduction is finally exposed, it is revealed through an avalanche of economic crises.

Thus we see that the source of economic crises lies in the capitalist system itself and in the basic contradiction of capitalism in which production is social but means of production are privately owned. As long as capitalism exists, economic crises are bound to explode. To eliminate crises, the capitalist system must first be destroyed.

Marxist Theory of Economic Crises Demolishes All Fallacious Theories of the Bourgeoisie Designed to Conceal Crises

The bourgeoisie and its apologists harbor extreme fear and hatred of the scientific conclusions about capitalist economic crises reached by Marxism. They have racked their brains to fabricate various lies in a vain attempt to dissociate crises with the capitalist system in order to deceive the working people and maintain the capitalist exploitative system.' For example, some of them attribute the source of crises to "underconsumption" and propose to use "consumption stimulation" to eliminate crises. In fact, underconsumption by the laboring people did not come into existence after the appearance of capitalism. It has been in existence ever since the human society was divided into the exploiting and the exploited classes. But overproduction appears only in the capitalist society. It is, therefore, easy to see that economic crises cannot be explained by "underconsumption."

After the Second World War, the militarization of the national economy led to temporary false prosperity in some capitalist countries. The apologists of the bourgeoisie seemed to have a lifesaving straw. They made the nonsensical statement that "those who hold the view that the capitalist countries would in- * evitably run into great economic crises are all mistaken." They saw the increasing participation of the governments of capitalist states in national economic activities as being "automatic regulators" which would, to a certain extent, enable the development of the capitalist economy to "automatically tend toward stability." This is also a lie. We know that the capitalist state machinery serves the bourgeoisie. Whatever the bourgeois state does to militarize the national economy or to regulate economic life, it does through various measures in order to intensify the exploitation of the people so that the capitalist can get richer. As Lenin pointed out long ago: "Whether in the United States or

Germany, the result of 'regulating economic life' is to create military hard-labor camps for the worker (and part of the peasantry) and to build havens for the banker and the capitalist. The regulating measures of these countries consist in tightening the belt of the worker to the verge of starvation while on the other hand guaranteeing (using secret and reactionary bureaucratic methods) that capitalist profit is higher than before the war." (2) The regulation of economic life in the bourgeois countries has not only not made the capitalist economy "automatically tend toward stability," on the contrary, it has impoverished the laboring people and diminished the market while enriching the capitalists. The basic contradiction of capitalism has steadily intensified, and the economic crises of capitalism have become more serious.

The Worsening Tendency of Capitalist Economic Crises

Capitalist Economic Crises Explode Periodically

As long as the capitalist system exists, the basic contradiction of capitalism will play its role. Capitalist economic crises are not problems which break out once or twice, but inevitably appear periodically. Looking at history, we see that the first large-scale economic crisis appeared in 1825 in England. After that, economic crises appeared repeatedly in 1836, 1847, 1857, and 1867. They occurred on the average of once every ten years. After these, they continued to explode with ever greater severity.

The cycle of economic crisis is the period of time between two successive crises. It consists in general of the four phases of crisis, depression, recovery, and boom. Of these, the phase of crisis is basic. It is the end of the last cycle and the beginning of a new cycle.

The Crisis Phase: Crises often strike suddenly. Before their arrival, there is widespread false prosperity in the market, and "business is thriving" in various industries. Although production already exceeds actual needs, plants are still working at full speed to fill up the warehouses and meet orders because of the credit system and active speculative activities.

All of a sudden, an economic crisis arrives due to a dislocation in one of the links in the capitalist economy. Once overproduction in one field is revealed and sales become difficult, other fields are soon affected, leading to a chain reaction. For example, production cuts or suspension in the automobile industry due to overproduction inevitably affect the coal, electric power, and transportation industries. Commercial speculators who initially help boost the false prosperity now turn around to unload their stocks at reduced prices, thus worsening the situation. Now the warehouses are overstocked, sales are difficult, and prices drop rapidly. To arrest the drop of prices, the capitalist may even resort to destroying large quantities of commodities. Under the blow of slow sales and falling prices, many medium and small enterprises go bankrupt en masse, and many banks close down. Those plants which continue to operate reduce their scale of production. At this time, the number of unemployed workers from all industries rapidly increases, and the whole economic situation rapidly worsens.

The Depression Phase: After the stormy assaults in the crisis phase, the tide of insolvency among industrial and commercial enterprises subsides. Those enterprises which survive the crisis conduct their activities on a smaller scale. Although shops are brightly decorated and their salesmen shout loudly, business is still very poor. A large number of workers are still unemployed with no means of livelihood. Capitalist industry, commerce, and banking are in the doldrums. However, in this phase, social consumption is still carried on. Stockpiles of commodities, after much damage, are sold slowly at very low prices. Under the surface of the doldrums, factors promoting the recovery of production slowly accumulate.

The Recovery Phase: With the reduction in stockpiles, prices slowly recover, and profits increase gradually. The capitalists step up their exploitation of the worker on the one hand and improve techniques and purchase new equipment on the other. Thus, production in the first category such as electric power, iron and steel, and machine building is the first to expand step by step. Employment gradually increases in this category. And the increase in employment leads to an increase in demand for consumer goods, thus stimulating the development of production in the second category. In this way, production gradually recovers, and the number of unemployed decreases. The once depressed capitalist economy is again gradually on its way to recovery.

The Boom Phase: The basic characteristics of this phase are rapid sales of commodities in the market, high profit, quickening activities in production and exchange, and the revival of credit and speculative activities. There is widespread "prosperity" in the market. The capitalists all try hard to expand production. Thus, under the surface of widespread "prosperity," new factors for another crisis steadily accumulate. Engels described this lively phenomenon of the capitalist economy as:,T Motion is quickened; slow steps turn into quick steps. Industrial quick steps turn into running steps. Running steps in turn become a sprint in a handicapped race in industry, commerce, credit, and speculative activities. In the end, after several final, desperate jumps, it falls into an abyss of collapse." (3)

Crisis — depression — recovery — boom — crisis characterizes the cyclical nature of economic crises. It also manifests the cyclical nature of capitalist production. It shows that capitalist production cannot progress continuously, but can only advance on a zigzag course.

Capitalist Economic Crises Worsen Steadily

In the development process of capitalist production, economic crises repeatedly appear. But each crisis is not a simple recurrence of the previous crisis. Capitalist economic crises tend to worsen steadily. Especially after the Second World War, economic crises have become more frequent and more severe.

This is manifest in the following aspects:

First, the cycle of economic crises has shortened, and economic crises are becoming more frequent.

Before the Second World War, economic crises occurred once every ten years. In the twenty-odd years after the Second World War, the cycle of economic crisis shortened markedly.

Postwar Economic Crises – The United States

Crisi period	Manufacturing output				Highest unemployment (10,000 persons)	Number of bankruptcies during manufacturing production reduction (units)
	Highest before crisis	Lowest during crisis	Reduction (%)	Months of reduction		
First 1948-49	August 1948	July 1949	8.6	11	410	9,246
Second 1953-54	July 1953	April 1954	9.9	9	370	7,724
Third 1957-58	March 1957	April 1958	14.8	13	520	15,579
Fourth 1960-61	January 1960	January 1961	7.5	12	571	15,668
Fifth 1969-70	September 1969	November 1970	8.1	14	550	13,629

Postwar Economic Crises – Japan

Crisi period	Manufacturing output				Highest unemployment (10,000 persons)	Number of bankruptcies during manufacturing production reduction (units)
	Highest before crisis	Lowest during crisis	Reduction (%)	Months of reduction		
First 1953-54	December 1953	August 1954	5.0	8	68	565
Second 1957-58	July 1957	June 1958	10.7	11	92	1,565
Third 1962	January 1962	December 1962	2.7	11	62	1,653
Fourth 1964-65	December 1964	May 1965	2.0	5	54	2,464
Fifth 1970-71	July 1970	May 1971	5.7	10	80	8,427

We can clearly see from the following tables that after the Second World War there were five economic crises in the United States and Japan. The average time between the first and the fifth crisis was less than five years in the United States and less than four years in Japan. After the Second World War, the cycle of economic crises markedly shortened because, under the rule of monopoly capital, the laboring people are subject to increasing exploitation, their purchasing power is reduced relatively, and problems of the domestic market are intensified. Furthermore, because of the external aggression and expansion of various imperialist countries, the contradictions between imperialism and the people of colonies and satellite countries are intensified. This promotes national revolutions in the colonies and satellite countries and consequently reduces the size of the foreign markets. Sales become a chronic problem. Thus, the contradiction between production and consumption is steadily intensified. All these show that the basic contradictions of capitalism are becoming ever more acute, and the capitalist production relation imposes an ever more serious obstacle to the development of the productive forces.

Second, the blind replacement of fixed capital makes the ratio of capitalist reproduction more out of balance. Before the Second World War, whenever economic crises exploded, investment in fixed capital usually dropped rapidly. However, after the Second World War, investment in fixed capital was generally higher than before the war. Even during crises, the level of investment still remained relatively high. In the fifth economic crisis in the United States after the war, investment in fixed capital not only did not fall, it went up instead. There was an increase of 3.5 percent between 1969 and 1970. In the fifth economic crisis in Japan after the war, investment in fixed capital in 1971 was 3.2 percent higher than in 1970.

The higher level of investment in fixed capital after the war shows that, on the one hand, the monopoly bourgeoisie uses the state machinery to increase its exploitation of the laboring people and transforms the surplus value extracted from the worker into capital. This speeds up capital accumulation but also speeds up the impoverishment of the proletariat and further reduces the purchasing power of the people. On the other hand, it shows that investment in fixed capital in the United States after the war consisted primarily of military orders and demands related to armaments and war preparations. Not only was a large amount of social resources wasted, but also the first category of industries was expanded without any control.

As a result, the ratio of social reproduction was even more out of balance, and the contradiction of capitalist reproduction became more acute. And capitalist economic crises became more frequent and more severe.

Third, manufacturing crises are interwoven and interact with agricultural crises, intensifying the whole economic crisis. Under the capitalist system, economic crises occur not only in manufacturing but also in agriculture. When agricultural crises explode, they are reflected in rapidly increasing stocks in the warehouse of the agricultural capitalist, falling wholesale prices, shrinking cultivated acreage, increasing unemployment of agricultural workers, falling wages among those still employed, and mass bankruptcy among individual farmers. It can be seen that agricultural crises, like manufacturing crises, arise because of overproduction and are caused by the basic contradiction of capitalism. As long as the capitalist system exists, agricultural overproduction crises are just as inevitable as manufacturing overproduction crises.

But, compared with manufacturing crises, agricultural crises last much longer. In the twenty-three years since the agricultural crisis exploded with the manufacturing crisis in 1948, agriculture has never been able to free itself from overproduction.

The intertwining and interaction between industrial and agricultural crises has become a serious problem in the postwar United States economy. Manufacturing crises lead to insolvency in a large number of enterprises, production cutbacks, unemployment, and falling wages. As a result, demand for agricultural products is reduced, aggravating the crisis of agricultural overproduction. At the same time, agricultural crises also damage agricultural production and impoverish agricultural laborers. Consequently, demand for agricultural means of production and manufacturing products is reduced and crises of manufacturing overproduction are intensified. Under the influence of manufacturing and agricultural crises, capitalist economic crises inevitably worsen.

Fourth, the crisis of capitalist overproduction is interwoven with the fiscal and financial crisis. After the Second World War, at the same time when the cycle of capitalist economic crises shortened, the explosion of fiscal and financial crises became more frequent. Fiscal and financial crises often occur along with economic crises. Fiscal and financial crises, like economic crises, are an inevitable result of a further intensification of the basic contradiction of capitalism. Their major features are: budgetary deficits, indiscriminate expansion of money supply, rising prices, balance-of-payments deficits, dwindling gold reserves, and currency devaluation.

After the Second World War, in order to free themselves of the worsening economic crises, the imperialist powers vainly attempted to resort to armament and war preparations to stimulate national economic growth. However, military expenses and production expenses of the defense industry rose steadily, leading to chronic budget deficits. To pay for the hugh defense expenses, imperialist countries have tried hard to increase taxation, negotiate foreign loans, issue currency, and engineer inflation, leading to fiscal crises. From the fiscal year 1946 to 1971, the United States budget deficits amounted to 137.9 billion dollars. The public debt reached 424.1 billion dollars. Even United States government officials claimed in dismay that the,T United States public debt was larger than those of all other countries combined." 'Tf we converted these public debts into United States one dollar notes, they could form a belt 35 feet wide encircling the equator 1,520 times."

As inflation worsens, the value of money falls steadily, leading to ever-rising prices. In the past, before the explosion of an economic crisis, in general the price level would fall.

But since the Second World War, the capitalist countries have been bent on adopting the militarization of the national economy and have pursued a policy of inflation. As a result, prices not only have not fallen during crises, but have gone up instead.

For example, there have been five economic crises in the United States since the Second World War. With the exception of the crisis in the 1948-49 period, prices in the other four periods all rose. This indicated that purchasing power fell. The devaluation of a currency inside a country inevitably affects its external credit standing. United States imperialism launched successive aggressive wars. With large increases in the army stationed overseas and in military expenditures, the huge outflow of United States dollars sent its international credit standing plummeting. Since the Second World War, financial crises have occurred repeatedly in the financial market of the capitalist world. Massive sales of United States dollars and rushes for gold have forced the United States government to devaluate the dollar twice: once at the end of 1971 and again in February 1973. The hegemony of the United States dollar in the capitalist world has disintegrated.

The concurrence of economic and financial crises has bogged down the capitalist economy in a deep quagmire. On the one hand, economic crises have led to a plunge in production and a steady impoverishment of the laboring people and have reduced the revenues of the capitalist countries, resulting in large deficits in federal budgets and in balance-of-payments which aggravate fiscal and financial crises. On the other hand, with the fiscal and financial crises worsening, inflation, higher taxation, falling real wages, and relative reduction in the purchasing power of the masses have inevitably further aggravated the economic crises of overproduction.

We can thus see that the cyclical nature of capitalist economic crises forms a vicious circle which gets worse and worse. The inherent antagonistic contradiction in capitalism is further intensified. Crises on top of crises have shaken the whole capitalist world like so many wild rainstorms.

Economic Crises Undermine the Basis of Capitalist Rule

Economic crises further intensify the basic contradiction of capitalism. During crises, competition among capitalists becomes more acute. Many medium and small enterprises, unable to compete with big enterprises, are the first to go bankrupt. To pay off their debts, many medium and small enterprises are forced to be auctioned off at losses. A few big enterprises which are more competitive take the opportunity to buy in at low prices. Therefore, after each crisis in the capi- talist society, capital becomes more concentrated in the hands of a few capitalists. Concentration of production and capital is hastened. The increasing concentration of production and capital implies that the basic contradiction of capitalism, namely, the contradiction between social production and capitalist private ownership, is becoming more acute.

Economic crises intensify class contradictions in the capitalist society. To reduce their own losses during crises, the capitalists inevitably take the knife to the laboring people. They dismiss workers en masse, cut wages, resort to inflation, increase taxation, and try their best to shift the burden of the crises onto the shoulders of the laboring people. At the same time, during crises, the exploitation of agriculture by capitalist manufacturing and of the rural areas by the urban areas also increases, resulting in mass bankruptcy among the peasants. Therefore, capitalist economic crises inflict severe hardship on the working class and other laboring people and intensify the contradiction between the workers and peasants on the one hand and the bourgeoisie and big landowners on the other, causing the proletariat's tide of struggle against the bourgeoisie to get higher and higher. Thus, the foundation of capitalist rule is continually rocked.

Economic crises fully expose the transitory nature of the capitalist system, revealing the existence of antagonistic contradictions between capitalist production relations and productive forces. The capitalist production relation is too confining for the huge social productive forces. It severely restricts the development of productive forces. During crises, only after immense destruction of productive forces and drastic reductions in production can the contradiction between production and consumption be temporarily and forcibly resolved. But at the same time, factors leading to another crisis are gradually accumulating. In the development process of the capitalist economy, there is a tendency for economic crises to get worse. This indicates that the capitalist production relation is decaying and must be replaced by another, new production relation which can adapt to the developmental needs of new productive forces, namely, the socialist production relation.

Major Study References
Engels, Anti-Duhring, pt. 3, chap. 2.
Lenin, "The Lessons of Crises," Complete Works of Lenin, Vol. 5.

Review Problems

1. What is the source of capitalist economic crisis?

2. Why do we say that economic crises hasten the downfall of capitalism?

Notes

1) Political Report to the Sixteenth Congress of the Central Committee of the Communist Party of the Soviet Union (Bolshevik)," Complete Works of Stalin, Vol. 12, p. 214.

2) "Where Is the Way Out in the Face of an Impending Catastrophe?" Complete Works of Lenin, Vol. 25, p. 324.

3) Engels, Anti-Duhring, Selected Works of Marx and Engels, Vol. 3, Jen-min ch'u-pan-she, 1972, p. 316.

9. The Unchanging Nature of Imperialism

Imperialism Is Monopoly Capitalism

Before the 1870s, capitalism was in a stage of free competition. From the 1870s onward, free competition steadily developed into monopoly. At the end of the nineteenth century and in the beginning of the twentieth century, capitalism completed its transition from free competition to monopoly and developed into imperialism. Lenin gave a complete and precise definition to imperialism: 'Imperialism is a special stage of capitalism. This special nature is manifested in three ways: (1) imperialism is monopoly capitalism; (2) imperialism is parasitic and decaying capitalism; and (3) imperialism is moribund capitalism." (1) This chapter first deals with the basic attributes of imperialism as monopoly capitalism.

Lenin pointed out that there are five basic characteristics in the economic aspect of imperialism. They are: "(1) production and capital concentration have been developed to such an extent that economic life is dominated by the monopoly organization; (2) banking capital and manufacturing capital have merged, and a financial oligarchy has emerged on the basis of this 'financial capital'; (3) capital export, as distinct from commodity export, assumes special significance; (4) an international monopoly alliance has been formed; and (5) the most powerful capitalist powers have dismembered the territories of the world." (2) Lenin's theory concerning imperialism is our telescope and microscope for understanding the reactionary nature of imperialism.

Monopoly Is the Deep-rooted Economic Basis of Imperialism

Monopoly Is an Inevitable Development of Capitalism

The transition from free competition to monopoly is the most marked economic phenomenon in the development of capitalism into imperialism. Other characteristics of imperialism are all related to monopoly and developed on the basis of monopoly. Therefore, imperialism is often known as monopoly capitalism. The birth of monopoly capitalism passed through three basic stages.

In the first stage in the 1860s and 1870s, free competition in capitalism reached its zenith of development. In manufacturing, the electric motor, the internal combustion engine, and a new steel-refining method were invented. The development of productive forces shifted the relative share of light and heavy industry in favor of heavy industry. With the development of heavy industry characterized by a higher organic composition of capital, concentration of capital was accelerated. Monopoly organizations began to emerge.

In the second stage after the explosion in 1873 of the most severe economic crisis in the nineteenth century, competition among enterprises became more acute. Many medium and small enterprises closed down, making way for the extensive development of monopoly organizations. In the United States, in 1879 Rockefeller set up the first trust (the Standard Oil Company). In 1880, the total production of anthracite coal was monopolized by seven companies. However, monopoly was still not in a dominant position. Most monopoly agreements were short-term and unstable. In the last thirty years of the nineteenth century, the steam turbine, the automobile, and the diesel locomotive were invented one after another. Productive forces were highly developed. The relative share of heavy industry was further increased. Conditions for a transition to the monopoly stage were basically completed.

In the third stage at the end of the nineteenth century and the beginning of the twentieth century, the accumulation and concentration of capital greatly accelerated. More and more capital was concentrated in the hands of big enterprises. Monopoly organizations rapidly developed to gain control over various major manufacturing sectors and formed the basis of all economic life. In the beginning of the twentieth century, United States monopoly organizations controlled 70 percent of the metallurgical industry, 66 percent of the iron and steel industry, 81 percent of the chemical industry, 85 percent of the aluminum production, 80 percent of the tobacco and sugar refining industries, and 95 percent of coal and oil production. From this time on, free competition capitalism grew into monopoly capitalism, and capitalism was transformed into imperialism. Hence, Lenin said, "Monopoly is the deep-rooted basis of imperialism." (3)

The transition from free competition capitalism to imperialism has not changed the fundamental nature of capitalism. Its economic basis is still capitalist private ownership of the means of production. Its class contradiction is still the contradiction between the proletariat and the bourgeoisie. Longstanding economic laws such as competition and chaotic production are still playing their active roles. Chairman Mao pointed out: "When the free competition stage in capitalism has developed into imperialism, the fundamental contradictions between the proletariat and the bourgeoisie, as well as the nature of the capitalist society, have not changed." (4) In the imperialist stage, some new features emerged, intensifying and magnifying the existing contradictions of capitalism.

Monopoly Organization Guarantees the Extraction of High Monopoly Profits

Monopoly organization is either the largest capitalist enterprise or an alliance of capitalist enterprises. They control the production and distribution of certain products and set monopoly prices by virtue of their monopoly position in order to extract high monopoly profits. The economic pulses of capitalist countries are under their manipulation.

Monopoly organizations assume many forms: some are "short-term price agreements" in which various enterprises collude to fix prices; some are "cartels" in which the enterprises are independent in production but have agreements concerning how to share the market, set up quotas, and fix prices; some are "syndicates" in which the enterprises are independent in production but cooperate in purchasing inputs and selling final products; others are "trusts" in which the enterprises producing identical goods merge; and some are "consortia" which consist of enterprises of different trades (manufacturing and mining, trading companies, transport and shipping companies, as well as banks). The development of monopoly organizations of various kinds gradually controls all economic sectors and the economic pulses of capitalist countries. Especially since the end of the Second World War, social production and social wealth have been increasingly concentrated in the hands of a few monopoly capitalists. This is manifested by:

1) A continuous expansion in the size of enterprises and increasing monopolization. Take the United States as an example. There was only one company with capital assets exceeding one billion dollars in 1901. In 1960, this had increased to 96 companies. In 1970, it had again increased to 282 companies.

2) Increasing control of industrial fields by a few monopoly capitalists. In many industrial fields, a few big companies control a major share of the production or even the whole production. In the United States, in 1969 the big automobile companies monopolized 78.1 percent of the nation's total automobile production. In England, in 1970 one iron and steel company monopolized 93 percent of the steel output. In Japan, in 1970 seven big monopoly organizations controlled 95.5 percent of the total shipbuilding tonnages of the country. In France, in 1968 one electric power company controlled the electric power generation for the whole country.

3) Increasing concentration and monopolization of agricultural production. In 1939, there were 6.097 million farms in the United States. In 1959, this was reduced to 3.701 million.

In 1971, only 2.800 million were left. An average of 90,000 farms went bankrupt each year. In fact, in the United States fewer than 50,000 big monopoly farms, or 2 percent of all the farms, produce and market more than 80 percent of the total United States agricultural produce.

4) Increasing diversification of the monopoly organization.

In the past, many companies produced only one or two products. But by the end of the 1960s, their operations extended to many areas. For example, the United States International Telephone and Telegraph Company was established in 1920. During the first forty years, its primary business was to manufacture telecommunications equipment. But during the last decade, it has purchased 50 companies unrelated to telecommunications equipment. Its operations have extended to bread, artificial fibers, construction, hotels, and insurance. It controls 150 companies all over the world, and its distribution networks have spread over more than 100 countries and regions.

Though there are differences among various forms of monopoly organization and further changes may develop, their nature is identical. They all seek to guarantee high monopoly profit to the monopoly capitalist by monopolizing production and markets.

High monopoly profit is profit well in excess of average profit which is obtained by the monopoly capitalist through his monopoly position. Where does high monopoly profit come from? It still comes from the surplus value created by the worker in the monopoly enterprise. The monopoly organization adopts various blood and sweat labor systems to increase labor intensity and exploit the worker. In addition, the monopoly capitalist also transfers part of the income of the worker and other people into his own hands by raising prices of consumer goods. Taking advantage of his monopoly position, the capitalist depresses the purchasing price of agricultural produce and raises the selling price of manufactured products to extract part of the value created by the peasant. Through monopoly pricing, he grabs part of the profit of the capitalists outside the monopoly organization. By nonequivalent exchanges, the monopoly capitalist plunders the people of colonies, satellites, and other countries. This shows that what the monopoly organization gains in the form of high monopoly profit is exactly what the worker, the small producer, and the people of colonies and satellites lose. A small part is extracted from nonmonopoly medium and small capitalists. From the viewpoint of the capitalist world as a whole, therefore, monopoly pricing has not changed the sum of the value nor the surplus value created in the capitalist world. In other words, monopoly pricing has operated within the sphere of the law of value; it has merely changed the form in which the law manifests itself. Similarly, the law of surplus value, the fundamental economic law of capitalism, is still functioning in the monopoly stage; only its effects and forms have changed. Prior to the monopoly stage, it was manifested through the average profit; in the monopoly stage, it is manifested through high profit.

The rising of monopoly profits implies that the working class and the laboring people are subject to increasingly heavier exploitation and that the exploitative measures of the monopoly capitalists have become more ruthless than ever before. From 1940 to 1949, the United States monopoly companies obtained an average of 24.356 billion dollars of high monopoly profit every year. From 1960 to 1969, this increased to 67.47 billion dollars. In Japan, the rate of surplus value in manufacturing amounted to 182 percent in 1930; it increased to 313 percent in 1954 and 345 percent in 1960. From these two sets of figures, we can see the acute polarization between the rich and the poor in the capitalist country.

Monopoly Leads to More Intense Competition

Free competition leads to monopoly. But monopoly cannot eliminate competition. On the contrary, it intensifies competition because competition is a product of capitalist private ownership. Monopoly has not changed the nature of capitalist private ownership and therefore cannot eliminate competition. This is especially true because means of production are increasingly concentrated in the hands of a few oligopolists. In order to eliminate their opponents, the monopoly organizations resort to any conceivable means to discourage their competitors. Competition becomes more acute and cruel. In the imperialist stage, life and death struggles among capitalists and capitalist cliques are manifested in the following ways:

Competition between monopoly organizations and nonmonopoly organizations. Under capitalist conditions, no matter how concentrated production is, it is impossible to achieve absolute monopoly. A certain number of nonmonopoly organizations always exists. Even in countries where monopoly capitalism is most developed, a large number of medium and small enterprises still exists. For example, in the United States, of her 4 million manufacturing enterprises, medium and small enterprises account for more than 3 million. Life and death struggles between monopoly and nonmonopoly enterprises are inevitable.

Intense competition also exists among monopoly organizations in their fight for sources of raw materials, markets, and transportation facilities.

There also exists among various enterprises in the same monopoly organization competition for markets and higher production and sales quotas. This kind of competition may even lead to the disintegration of some monopoly organizations and results in new monopoly organizations and new competition.

In trusts and consortia, the struggle among various big capitalists for leadership, stock control, and share of profits never ceases.

Therefore, monopoly capitalism is not "organized capitalism" as the bourgeoisie and the revisionists claim. On the contrary, monopoly intensifies competition and aggravates the capitalist contradiction between social production and private ownership and between the organized production of individual enterprises and the chaotic conditions of social production. Lenin pointed out long ago, "Monopoly arising from free competition cannot eliminate competition. It is superimposed on competition and coexists with competition, consequently leading to many very acute contradictions, frictions, and confrontations." (5) "The combination of the two contradicting 'principles' of competition and monopoly represents the true nature of capitalism. It is exactly this combination that leads to disintegration, namely socialist revolution.*' (6)

Financial Capital Is an Omnipotent Monopolist

Financial Capital Is Formed by a Merger of Banking Capital and Manufacturing Capital

The first economic attribute of imperialism is monopoly.

The second is the formation of financial capital and the rule of financial oligopoly. With the emergence of monopoly in manufacturing, monopoly also appears in the banking industry. When free competition is dominant, the bank serves as a middleman.

It pools idle funds in society for the use of manufacturing and commercial capitalists through short-term loans. With the arrival of the imperialist stage, the bank is transformed from a middleman into an all-powerful monopolist. Monopoly in the banking industry leads to a fundamental change in the relation between the bank and the manufacturing industry. Big banks infiltrate the manufacturing industry by purchasing manufacturing stocks. Manufacturing monopoly organizations infiltrate the banks by purchasing banking stocks. As a result, monopoly banking capital and monopoly manufacturing capital gradually merge to form financial capital. 'The concentration of capital; the development of monopoly from concentration; the merger between the banks and the manufacturing industry or their mixed growth — these are the origins of financial capital and the content of this concept." (7) "The characteristic of imperialism is not manufacturing capital, but financial capital." (8) The few largest capitalists who control a large amount of financial capital are the financial oligopolists. The chief means by which financial capital controls the national economy is the "participation system." Through a major joint-stock company ("mother company") which the financial capitalist controls, stocks of other joint-stock companies are purchased. Once their stocks are under control, they become "son companies." These "son companies" use the same method to control more "grandson companies." In this way, a relatively small amount of capital can control and manipulate capital many times the amount of the original capital. The national economy and most of the wealth created by the laboring people are thus under the control of a few financial oligopolists. In 1968, eighteen financial groups in the United States controlled capital assets worth 678.4 billion dollars. Of these, the Morgan and Rockefeller groups were the two biggest monopoly financial organizations. They had the most economic power and their influence covered the whole capitalist world. As of 1970, these two financial groups controlled capital assets totaling 330.4 billion dollars, representing about half of the capital assets controlled by the eighteen United States financial monopoly organizations and exceeding all the capital assets controlled by the financial monopoly organizations of England, France, Japan, and West Germany combined. Enterprises controlled by the Morgan group covered various departments of the national economy, especially basic industries such as iron and steel, electricity and gas, electronics, and chemicals. In public utilities and transportation, the Morgan group T s position was even stronger, playing a vital role in the United States economy. Enterprises controlled by the Rockefeller group were more concentrated. Its five major oil companies controlled 94.1 percent of the oil extraction in the United States in 1967. The two groups exercise a decisive influence in the United States economy.

Financial Capital Directly Controls State Political Power and Other Superstructures

Lenin pointed out, "Once monopoly is formed, controlling vast amounts of capital, it inevitably infiltrates into various aspects of society's life." (9) To further exploit and oppress the laboring people for high monopoly profit, financial capital seeks control not only of the economic lifeblood of the state but also of state political power. Financial oligopolists bribe high-level officials and state legislators to serve as their spokesmen for the control of the state machinery. Sometimes they personally occupy the leadership positions of the state.

Take the postwar Eisenhower administration as an example. Eisenhower came into power with the support of the Rockefeller and Morgan groups. Of the 272 high-level officials in his administration, 150 were big capitalists. Among them, Secretary of State Dulles was a trustee of the Rockefeller Foundation, Defense Secretary Wilson was a general manager of the General Motors Company, Gates, another defense secretary, was an important person in the Morgan group and served as the director of the Morgan Guaranty Trust Company in 1965, and Secretary of the Treasury Humphrey was a responsible official of the Han-na Mining Company which was a major enterprise of the Cleveland group. The financial oligopoly controlled not only state political power but also various spheres of the superstructure. The newspaper, publishing, broadcasting, television, and movie industries were all under the control of monopoly capital and financial oligopoly. The Rockefeller group also owned the largest "philanthropic enterprises," various foundations, learned societies, museums, hospitals, "welfare organizations," and "cultural" centers. These were all tools used by the Rockefeller financial group to expand into various aspects of social life.

State Monopoly Capitalism Pushes the Relation between Capital and Labor to the Ultimate

Engels once prophesied that when capitalism develops to a certain stage, "the real agent of the capitalist society, the state, must take the responsibility for managing production." (10) In the imperialist stage when the productive forces have been greatly developed, some monopoly capital groups are shown to be increasingly incapable of controlling the productive forces. Consequently, the phenomenon arises in which "the state merges ever closer with the alliance of capitalists which possesses enormous power. Its scandalous oppression of the laboring people becomes more severe." (11) This is state monopoly capitalism. State monopoly capitalism is monopoly capitalism based on capitalist ownership and the merger of monopoly capital with state political power.

The rapid development of state monopoly capitalism is a prominent feature of contemporary imperialism. Since the Second World War, imperialist countries have implemented so- called "nationalization" by having the state purchase private enterprises; or the state has invested directly in so-called "state enterprises." These state monopoly capitalist enterprises constitute a very high proportion of capitalist enterprises. In 1968, the share of state monopoly capitalist enterprises in four major countries in Western Europe was as follows:

Countries	Percentage share in staff and workers	Percentage share in assets
France	11.2	33.5
West Germany	8.7	22.7
Italy	11.6	28
United Kingdom	8.5	17

The development of United States state monopoly capitalism had its own characteristics. During the Second World War, the United States government established a large number of "state enterprises." After the war, they were sold to the monopoly capital groups at very low prices. At the same time, the United States government adopted the "blood transfusion" technique of supporting the monopoly capital groups by means of taxes extracted from the people.

The services rendered by the imperialist countries to the monopoly bourgeoisie, in addition to "nationalization" and "state enterprises," assumed the following forms, assuring the monopoly groups high monopoly profits: (1) Using federal treasury funds and the people's taxes to subsidize the capitalists when they undertook the risks of investment; (2) redistributing a large part of the national income in favor of the monopoly capital organization through state legislation and budgets;

(3) creating facilities conducive to the monopoly capitalist's concentration and accumulation of capital and to his absorption of medium and small enterprises; and (4) though the means by which the imperialist countries serve their monopoly bourgeoisie are different, their objective is always the same, namely, the strengthening of the capitalist enslavement of the proletariat. "The more of the productive forces which the bourgeois state takes into its possession, the more it becomes a truly total capitalist, and the more it exploits the people. The worker is still a hired laborer and a proletarian. The capitalist relation has not only not been eliminated, it has been elevated to its ultimate." (12)

Contrary to the claims of the bourgeois apologists and the modern revisionists, state monopoly capitalism does not have any "socialist element" which can exercise planned leadership over the national economy. On the contrary, state monopoly capitalism has not changed the capitalist nature of production relations a bit. It is merely a tool of the imperialist countries to serve the monopoly organization and strengthen the rule of the financial oligopoly. State monopoly capitalism strengthens the exploitation of the working class and the laboring people by monopoly capital, strengthens the plunder of the people of the colonies by monopoly capital, accelerates armament and war preparations, and intensifies competition and chaos so that the inherent contradiction in the capitalist society becomes more acute. It runs into increasing opposition from the proletariat and the broad laboring people and, at the same time, goes a step further in preparing the material conditions for the proletarian revolution.

Capital Export Leads to World Domination by Financial Capital

Capital Export Is an Indication of Relative Capital Surplus

"The characteristic of the old capitalism in which free competition was dominant is commodity export. The characteristic of the newest capitalism in which monopoly is dominant is capital export." (13) Capital export exists in the premonopoly stage of capitalism; but it is widespread and significant only in the stage of monopoly capitalism. This is because the cruel exploitation of the domestic laboring people by the monopoly organization in the imperialist countries helps accumulate a large amount of capital. However, since almost all profitable business has already been monopolized inside the country and high monopoly profit cannot be guaranteed in other, less developed, domestic sectors, a large amount of accumulated capital thus becomes "surplus capital." Where can profitable outlets be found for this "surplus capital"? In those developing countries where capital is scarce, wages are low, land and raw materials are cheap, and high profit can be obtained. Therefore, capital is exported for high monopoly profits through direct investment (mining, manufacturing, railroads, shops) and indirect investment (loans), greedily exploiting the broad laboring people of the developing countries. Capital export has developed rapidly only since the beginning of the twentieth century. In 1970, the total capital export from major capitalist countries reached more than 300 billion dollars, an increase of more than five times over that of 1914.

Capital Export Is an Imperialist Tool to Exploit and Oppress the People of Various Countries

In the search for monopoly profits and external expansion, capital export is an important tool used by the monopoly capitalist to exploit and plunder the people of various countries, especially the peoples of the developing Asian, African, and Latin American countries. Take old China as an example. On the eve of the Anti-Japanese War, foreign capital in China totaled 4.3 billion dollars. Near the end of the war, it increased to 9.8 billion dollars, of which, the share of investment by Japanese imperialism was the highest, amounting to 6 billion dollars. This foreign capital controlled 70 percent of China's modern industry and transportation, 95 percent of the iron and steel and petroleum industries, 75 percent of the electric power and coal industry. More than half of the food processing industry was operated by foreign capital. In 1945, after imperialist Japan surrendered, United States imperialism replaced Japanese imperialism as the dominant power in China. In 1948, the American imperialist investment in China (including so-called "United States aid") represented 80 percent of foreign investment in China. The invasion of foreign capitalism "not only played a role in undermining China's feudal economic basis, but also created certain objective conditions and possibilities for the development of capitalist production in China." (14) However, "the purpose of the imperialist powers in invading China was definitely not to transform feudal China into a capitalist China. Their purpose was just the opposite. They wanted to transform China into their semicolony or colony." (15) The influx of a large amount of foreign capital on a long-term basis seriously undermined the social productive forces of China and brought extreme poverty to the livelihood of the Chinese people, reducing China to a semicolonial and semifeudal status.

After the Second World War, there was a large increase of capital export from the capitalist countries, and the United States became the largest capital-exporting country. In 1914, the United States exported only 3.5 billion dollars of capital. In 1970, it rapidly rose to 155.5 billion dollars, an increase of more than forty-three times in fifty-six years. With the rapid increase in capital export, there were also large increases in the high monopoly profits of the monopoly capitalists. From 1950 to 1970, the profit from United States private direct investment in foreign countries amounted to 88.77 billion dollars, or 14 percent higher than the total United States private direct investment in foreign countries up to the end of 1970. Profit from investments made by imperialism in Asia, Africa, and Latin America was astonishingly high. For example, in 1970 United States direct investment in Asia, Africa, and Latin America accounted for 27.3 percent of her total foreign direct investment. In the same year, profit extracted from Asia, Africa, and Latin America accounted for 43.5

percent of the total profit from all foreign direct investment. At the present time, imperialism has become the greediest bloodsucker of the people over a large area of the world.

After the Second World War, in addition to further developing private capital export, the imperialist countries paid increasing attention to state capital export. The major form of this state capital export was foreign "aid." From mid-1945 to mid-1971, the total amount of United States foreign aid reached 149.6 billion dollars. This foreign "aid" was classified into so-called "grants" and "loans." "Grants" were nominally free; but in fact, they were the strings by which the grantee countries were controlled. Chairman Mao long ago exposed the reactionary political objective of United States imperialist "aid": "Gifts, yes; but with conditions. What conditions? You have to follow my footsteps." (16) In recent years, the proportion of loans from the imperialist countries is increasing, and the proportion of "grants" is correspondingly decreasing. These so-called loans all have interest rates exceeding 5 percent per annum. The highest rate reached 8 percent per annum. In addition, many political, economic, and military strings are attached. It is not only a bloodsucking straw but is also an important tool for the implementation of the aggressive and expansionary policies of imperialism and the fight for world hegemony.

Capital export from the imperialist countries inflicts severe hardships on the colonial and semicolonial countries and their people. However, the imperialists and revisionists try their best to defend these aggressive acts. They claim that capital export can "help" the economically underdeveloped countries to reach economic prosperity. The Soviet revisionist renegades even unabashedly suggested that imperialism could spend all the money saved through total disarmament to "help" the economically underdeveloped countries in Asia, Africa, and Latin America create a new era. All nations and people of the world who have been subject to exploitation and slavery have had their full share of the hardship brought about by the so-called "aid" of imperialism. The market is shrinking for such arguments of the Soviet revisionist renegades.

The International Monopoly Alliance Carved up the World Economically

The International Monopoly Alliance Is a Supermonopoly

The monopoly organizations of a country first carve up the domestic market. Under capitalism, the domestic market is closely related to the foreign market. With increasing capital export and the expansion of the international association and the sphere of influence of the largest monopoly alliance, a few large monopoly organizations of several countries can control most of the world's production and distribution of some commodities. These large monopoly organizations are comparable in power and may, out of self-interest and under certain conditions, make temporary international agreements and form alliances to set international monopoly prices, divide up sources of raw materials and distribution markets, limit production quotas, and thus form an international monopoly organization. These monopoly organizations have already exceeded the boundary of one country. Lenin called them "supermonopolies."

These super monopoly organizations appeared as early as the 1870s and developed rapidly in the twentieth century. After the Second World War, new international monopoly organizations were formed, and some old international monopoly organizations disintegrated. According to statistics, up to 1968 the total foreign capital assets (accounting value) of international monopoly companies amounted to 94 billion dollars. The annual production value of their foreign subsidiary companies was 240 billion dollars. The five largest international monopoly organizations were: the General Motors Company, the New Jersey Standard Oil Company, the Ford Motor Company, the British-Dutch Shell Oil Company, and the General Electric Company. As a result of the rapid development of international monopoly companies, the monopoly financial groups' monopoly of world production and trade is strengthened. Some manufacturing fields in the capitalist world such as rubber tires, oil, tobacco, pharmaceuticals, and automobiles are almost completely controlled by international monopoly organizations. In recent years, there have been new developments in regional international monopoly alliances. The Common Market and the European Free Trade Area of Western Europe are, economically speaking, regional international monopoly alliances of sorts. Their development and expansion provide checks and balances to the vain attempts of the United States and the Soviet Union to divide up the world.

The Struggle among International Monopoly Alliances Is Intensifying

In the imperialist stage, the enormous development of monopoly organizations requires more supplies of resources and markets for commodities and more areas for capital investment. Take 1969 for instance: the proportion of raw materials which the United States imported from Asia, Africa, and Latin America was as follows: tin ore, close to 100 percent; manganese ore, 91.9 percent; copper ore, 78.2 percent; petroleum, 62.9 percent; chromium and others, 41.6 percent. The proportion of raw material imports by Japan, West Germany, and the United Kingdom from Asia, Africa, and Latin America was also high. The struggle for sources of raw material supply among international monopoly organizations, therefore, has become increasingly severe. To fight for oil in the Middle East, the monopoly capitalists of many countries tried very hard to get into this area, and consequently, the struggle was especially acute and complex.

The struggle among the monopoly organizations of various countries for markets to sell commodities is also very acute. After the Second World War, the United States dominated the capitalist world market for some time. Her total volume of exports accounted for one-third of the total capitalist world exports. But with the rising economic power of Western Europe and Japan, the United States hegemony began to decline. In 1971, her share of the capitalist world exports was reduced to only 14.2 percent. In Asia, Africa, and Latin America, the monopoly organizations of Western Europe, North America, and Australasia repeatedly engaged in intense struggle for markets. Faced with the influx of Japanese automobiles on the West Coast of the United States, Henry Ford II, the president of the Ford Motor Company, lamented: "This is only the beginning. These Japanese will soon invade the heart of America." Lenin pointed out profoundly: "The dismembering of the world among the capitalists is not due to their specific vicious character. Rather, it occurs because concentration has reached such a stage that they cannot but take this path to obtain profit." (17)

The international monopoly alliance is originally an international monopoly organization set up by the monopoly capitalists of various countries to divide up the world market for high monopoly profits. But agreements and alliances among the monopoly capitalists of various countries to divide up the world are at best temporary and relative. Their pursuit of high monopoly profits guarantees that the struggle among them will go on for - ever. Imperialism and revisionism hold that the internationalization of capital will bring the possibility of peace to nations. This wishful thinking has been sharply criticized by Lenin.

Lenin pointed out: 'The form of struggle among international monopoly organizations may change frequently for various comparatively local and temporary reasons. But the nature of the struggle and the class content of the struggle will never change as long as classes exist." (18) The history of the last half- century or so has fully confirmed Lenin's scientific judgment.

Competition among the Imperialist Powers for the Division and Redivision of the World

Colonies Are Important Conditions for the Existence of Imperialism

In the imperialist era, the economic division of the world by monopoly capital must inevitably be followed by the territorial division of the world into colonies. The implementation of the colonial policy and the seizure of colonies began in the stage of primitive accumulation. But only in the imperialist stage is the "climax" of struggle for colonies begun, and the struggle to divide the world's territories among imperialist countries intensified. This is because:

First, colonies are the most important source of raw materials for imperialism. Monopoly leads to large-scale production. The larger the scale of production, the more raw materials are needed, and the more important it is to control the sources of raw materials. Lenin pointed out, "The more advanced capitalism is, the scarcer raw materials are, and the more acute the struggle for the world's sources of raw materials becomes, the more intense the struggle to colonize is." (19)

Second, colonies are the most profitable outlets for the capital exports of imperialism. In colonies, the monopoly organizations of the suzerain can exploit and enslave the laboring people more ruthlessly. They can more easily eliminate competitors through monopolistic means and guarantee high monopoly profits for the exported capital.

Third, colonies are the most profitable sales market for the monopoly organizations. The suzerain can use protective tariffs to guarantee their monopolist position.

Fourth, colonies are also military strategic bases in the struggle for world hegemony among imperialist countries. The suzerain can establish a large number of military bases there, plunder large quantities of strategic materials, and recruit large numbers of soldiers to serve the military policies of imperialism.

In sum, colonies are important conditions for the existence of imperialism. "Only by occupying colonies can the triumph of the monopoly organization be fully secured." (20) Therefore, the imperialist countries are always fighting for more colonies. After the 1870s, the struggle to divide the world's territories among the imperialist powers reached an extremely acute degree. Up to 1914, the colonies occupied by England, Russia, France, Germany, the United States, and Japan reached 65 million square kilometers, and they ruled 523 million people. Among them, the area of the colonies owned by the czar of Russia was second only to that of England. At that time, out of Russia's 22.8 million square kilometers, 17.4 million square kilometers were colonies. Lenin pointed out clearly, 'The czarist government expressed more vividly than other national governments the reactionary nature of war, plundering, and enslaving peoples." (21) Czarist Russia was the "prison of various nationals." (22)

China had long been fiercely carved up by the imperialist powers. From the latter part of the nineteenth century, the imperialist countries who invaded China marked out their respective spheres of influence according to their economic and military power in China and reduced her to a semicolony. For example, the provinces in the middle and lower reaches of the Yangtze River were under British influence;

Yunnan, Kwang- tung, and Kwangsi provinces were under French influence. After the Russo-Japanese War in 1905, the southern part of northeast China was brought under Japanese influence. In the process of imperialism's slaughter of China, czarist Russia was the first "to stretch out her grisly hands." (23) The old czar invaded China 'like a thief' (24) and occupied more than 1.5 million square kilometers of Chinese territory, equal to three times the area of France or twelve times that of Czechoslovakia.

The Division and Redivision of Colonies Inevitably Leads to Wars

To obtain high monopoly profits, imperialism must engage in aggression and expansion and fight for the division and redivision of world territories. The outcome of such competition is determined by the relative strength of the imperialist countries. The mightiest holds world hegemony. The highest form of resolving conflicts through strength is war. As long as imperialism exists, wars are inevitable. Imperialism fights for colonies and world hegemony and obtains high monopoly profits through wars. Lenin pointed out, "Modern wars are created by imperialism." (25) The two world wars in the first half of the twentieth century were caused by the division and redivision of the world and the struggle for world hegemony among the imperialist powers.

Economic monopoly inevitably intensified the fundamental contradictions of imperialism and accentuated the political and economic crises of capitalism. To free themselves from political and economic crises, to reduce domestic class contradictions, and to save the capitalist system, the imperialist powers ran the risk of wars, engaging in moribund struggles. Chairman Mao pointed out, "The outbreak of imperialist world wars was an attempt by the imperialist countries to extricate themselves from new economic and political crises." (26)

Once we understand the economic reality of imperialism, we will understand Lenin's famous statement that "on the economic basis of private ownership of means of production, imperialist wars are inevitable." (27) United States imperialism prospered through wars. In the two world wars, the United States monopoly organization engaged in large-scale rearmament transactions and obtained windfall gains from wars. In the First World War, United States monopoly capitalists obtained 38 billion dollars as windfall profit; in the Second World War, they obtained 117 billion dollars as windfall profit and became the dominant power in the capitalist world. From then on, the United States monopoly bourgeoisie looked all the more to wars as shortcuts to prosperity and continuously waged aggressive wars. According to statistics, in the aggressive war in Korea, United States monopoly capital obtained 115.4 billion dollars as a windfall profit; in the aggressive war in Vietnam, in 1964 and 1965 alone, the windfall profit amounted to 76 billion dollars. Every dollar in the pocket of the United States millionaires is stained with the blood of the laboring people. As long as imperialism exists, the source of modern wars exists. To eliminate wars, we must eliminate the imperialist system.

However, the imperialist and revisionist always fabricate all sorts of nonsense to deceive the people in order to protect the imperialist system. A typical absurdity is found in On Super- i mperialism, a work which the chief of the Second International, Kautsky, fabricated on the eve of the First World War. Pur- posedly overlooking the fact that the external expansion and aggression of imperialism are determined by the substance of monopoly capitalism, he vigorously contended that those were the imperialists' conscious policies. Hence, he alleged: "These policies of neosuperimperialism would replace international financial struggles with international cooperation to exploit the world." As a result, a permanent peace would emerge. Pointedly exposing this fallacy, Lenin asserted: "Kautsky's On Super - imperialism is aimed at creating an illusion that permanent peace could be achieved under capitalism. It is an extremely reactionary idea attempting to dupe the masses; it is a means to detract people's attention from contemporary acute contradictions and outstanding problems to an illusory future of the so-called 'neosuperimperialism. 1 " (28) Since the fabrication of Kautsky*s On Superimperialism, all revisionists have treated it as a most valuable treasure. They repeatedly propagated this "theory" under different guises and conditions. Modern Soviet Russian revisionists headed by Brezhnev described certain relative, temporary agreements between the two contemporary superpowers as so-called "structures for permanent peace," vainly attempting to conceal the deep-seated contradictions between them and to deceive the people and tranquilize the opposite side in order to facilitate their own imperialist expansion.

Within imperialism, there is both competition and collusion. Collusion is for the purpose of larger competition. Competition is absolute and long term, and collusion is relative and temporary. Temporary agreements today set the stage for larger competition tomorrow.

Monopoly is the most deep-seated economic basis of imperialism. It determines the aggressive and plundering nature of imperialism and will not change. Just as Chairman Mao pointed out: "When we say that 'imperialism is very dangerous,' we mean that its nature cannot change. Imperialist elements will never put down their weapons or transform themselves into Buddhas until their extinction." (29)

Major Study References

Lenin, Imperialism, the Highest Stage of Capitalism, chaps. 1 - 6.

Chairman Mao, "On New Democracy."

Chairman Mao, "Cast Away Illusions and Prepare for Struggle."

Review Problems

1. What are the basic characteristics of imperialism? Why do we say monopoly is the most deep-seated economic basis of imperialism?

2. Why do we say the nature of imperialism will never change? Criticize On Superimperialism and its disguised versions.

Notes

1) 'Imperialism and the Split in the Socialist Movement," S elected Works of Lenin, Vol. 2, Jen-min ch'u-pan-she, 1972, p. 883.

2) Ibid., p. 808.

3) Ibid., p. 817.

4) "On Contradiction," Selecte d Work s of Mao Tse-tung, Vol. 1, Jen-min ch'u-pan-she, 1968, p. 289.

5) Imperialism, the Highest Stage of Capitalism, Selected Works of Lenin, Vol. 2, Jen-min ch'u-pan-she, 1972, ppT807-08.

6) "Materials for the Amendment of the Party Charter," Complete Works of Lenin, Vol. 24, pp. 431-32.

7) Imperialism, the Highest Stage of Capitalism,

Selec ted Works of Lenin, Vol. 2, Jen-min ch'u-pan-she, 1972, p. 769.

8) Ibid., p. 810.

9) Ibid., p. 779.

10) Engels, Anti-Duhring, Selected W orks of Marx and Engels, Vol. 3, Jen-min ch'u-pan-she, 1972, p. 317.

11) State and Revolution, Selected Works of Lenin,

Vol. 3, Jen-min ch'u-pan-she, 1972, p. 171.

12) Engels, Anti-Duhring, Sel ected Wo rk s of Marx and Engels, Vol. 3, Jen-min ch'u-pan-she, 1972, p. 318.

13) Imperialism, the Highest Stage of Capitalism,

Selected Works of Leni n, Vol. 2, Jen-min ch'u-pan-she, 1972, p. 782.

14) "The Chinese Revolution and the Chinese Communist Party," Selected Works of Mao Tse-tung, Vol. 2, Jen-min ch'u-pan- she, 1968, p. 589.

15) Ibid., p. 591.

16) "Farewell, Leighton Stuart!" Sele cted Works of Mao Tse-tung, Vol. 4, Jen-min ch'u-pan-she, 1968, p. 1384.

17) I mperialism, the Highe st Sta ge of Capitalism,

Selected Works of Lenin, Vol. 2, Jen-min ch'u-pan-she, 1972, p. 795.

18) Ibid., p. 795.

19) Ibid., pp. 802-03.

20) Ibid., p. 802.

21) "Socialism and War," Co mplete W o rks of Lenin, Vol. 21, pp. 313-14.

22) "The Revolutionary Proletariat and National Self- Determination," Complete Works of Lenin, Vol. 21, p. 392.

23) "Chinese Wars," C omplete Work s of Lenin, Vol. 4, p. 335.

24) Ibid., p. 336.

25) "Draft Decisions of the Left Zimmerwaldists," Complete Works of Lenin, Vol. 21, p. 324.

26) "The Current Situation and the Party's Tasks," Selected Works of Mao Tse-tung, Vol. 2, Jen-min ch'u-pan-she, 1968, p. 578.'

27) "Preface to the French and German Editions of Imperi

alism, the High est Stag e of Capitalism," Select ed Works

of Lenin, Vol. 2, Jen-min ch'u-pan-she, 1972, p. 733.

28) Imperialism, the Highest Stage of Capitalism,

Selected Wor ks of Lenin, Vol. 2, Jen-min ch'u-pan-she, 1972, p. 836.

29) "Cast Away Illusions and Prepare for Struggle," Selected

Works of Mao Tse-tung, Vol. 4, Jen-min ch'u-pan-she, 196$,

pp. 1375-7 6^

10. Imperialism is the Eve of Proletarian Socialist Revolution

Imperialism Is Decaying and Moribund Capitalism

After capitalism develops from free competition to the monopoly stage, its various contradictions intensify. These contradictions, like volcanos, threaten the existence of imperialism. The life of imperialism is then limited. Despite its fierce facade, imperialism is a paper tiger. Imperialism is the eve of socialist revolution.

Imperialism Is Parasitic or Decaying Capital ism

The Stagnating Tendency of the Development of Production and Technology

When capitalism develops into imperialism, it begins to decay and decline. Imperialism is parasitic or decaying capitalism. The decaying nature of imperialism is brought about by monopoly rule. Monopoly is the economic basis of the decaying nature of imperialism.

The decaying nature of imperialism is primarily manifested in the serious obstruction of the development of productive forces by the monopoly organization. It artificially prevents technical progress and ushers a stagnating tendency into the development of production and technology. Before monopoly, the capitalist cannot neglect technological advancement in his pursuit of excess profits at the expense of his competitors. In the monopoly stage, because the monopoly capitalist controls an absolute majority of some production sectors, he can obtain high monopoly profits by setting monopoly prices. Thus, the motive to adopt advanced technology is weakened to a certain degree. Under monopoly rule, the capitalist is afraid that advanced technology may weaken his monopoly position. He often artificially obstructs the development of new technology.

Why is the monopoly capitalist so afraid of advanced technology and why does he obstruct it? First, the widespread adoption of new technology and new equipment almost certainly reduces the cost of products and increases output. But it will also result in capital loss or the obsolescence of his original machines and equipment and bring about invisible depreciation; second, the adoption of new technology and equipment will lead to competition from similar and cheaper commodities which may threaten his monopoly position. The monopoly capitalist often reduces production to maintain monopoly prices and extract high monopoly profits. Therefore, many new techniques and inventions beneficial to the development of production are put aside once their patents have been bought by the monopoly capitalist. For example, the technology of artificial petroleum is detrimental to the monopoly of the petroleum companies and has been put aside for exactly twenty years. The invention of atomic energy is a great scientific achievement, but it is used by imperialism to make atomic weapons for aggression and not fully used as motive power for industry.

The obstruction of the development of production and technology by monopoly results in a gradual decline in the rate of capitalist expanded reproduction. Take the United States as an example. Its industrial production increased by about 3.9 times during the thirty years from 1871 to 1900. But in the thirty years [sic] from 1901 to 1929, it increased by only 2.7 times. In the thirty years from 1930 to 1959, the average (annual) rate of increase in industrial production was only 4.4 percent. The decreasing rate of development in United States production fully exposes the decaying nature of imperialism.

The appearance of a stagnating and decaying tendency in the development of production and technology in the imperialist stage does not mean that the development of production technology in the imperialist countries has come to a standstill. Lenin pointed out: "Should we think that this decaying tendency precludes any rapid development of capitalism, we would be mistaken. No, in the imperialist phase, individual industrial fields, individual bourgeois classes or strata, and individual countries will manifest in different degrees first this tendency and then that tendency." (1) This is because free competition leads to monopoly. But monopoly by no means eliminates competition.

It only makes competition more acute or ruthless. In competition, various monopoly capital groups adopt violence, bribery, deception, and fraud to eliminate competitors. At the same time, the relative economic strength among various major capitalist countries may change. Under the general tendency of frustrated development of productive forces, the position of some capitalist countries may deteriorate, but the position of others may improve. Therefore, in the monopoly stage, the development of production and technology in the imperialist countries suffers a general stagnating tendency. But this by no means precludes the possibility of more rapid development in the production technology of a particular period, individual, or sector.

In the imperialist phase, the production technology of individual countries may undergo more rapid development. But, it is often temporary and exceptional. Take Japan as an example. In the 1950-1971 period, Japan's national product increased by an average annual rate of more than 10 percent. This trend cannot long be maintained. This faster development of Japan's production was a result of substantial help from United States imperialism to the monopoly capital of Japan. The aggressive wars against Korea and Vietnam by United States imperialism brought windfall profits to the monopoly capitalists of Japan. During the aggressive war against Korea in the 1950-53 period, United States imperialism paid Japan at least 2 billion dollars for military "special needs" orders. During the aggressive war against Vietnam, United States imperialism's payment to Japan for "special needs" amounted to 300-400 million dollars per year in the first half of the 1960s. From 1965 onward, it increased to 500-600 million dollars per year. United States imperialism also gave large quantities of loans to the monopoly capital of Japan, invested directly in Japan's heavy industry, and exported a large number of technical patents to Japan. At the same time, Japanese monopoly capital cruelly exploited the domestic laboring people and received large amounts of subsidies from the state budget. All these also contributed to the fast development of Japan's industry. The undervalued Japanese yen made Japanese goods very competitive in the world market. The above shows that the factors that promoted the development of Japan's industry cannot last long. The fast development of the Japanese economy is not only temporary but also abnormal and without foundations. First, along with the blind development of Japanese industry, agricultural production steadily declined. After the Second World War, the production of wheat cereals in Japan plummeted, the production of beans decreased substantially, and rice production has declined since 1968. From 1960 to 1970, the self-sufficiency rate of Japan's food products fell from 90 percent to 73 percent. Second, raw materials are largely imported and commodities depend heavily on the export market. The import ratio of ten major items of raw materials, including copper, aluminum, iron ore, petroleum, and coal, was 71 percent in 1960 and increased to 90 percent in 1970. The export ratio of Japanese industrial products increased from 18.3 percent in 1950 to 30.1 percent in 1969, including 46.4 percent of synthetic fiber woven goods, 67.4 percent of sewing machines, and 68.9 percent of ships. These facts show that the foundation of Japan's economic development is very shaky.

It is impossible to sustain development at present rates on a long-term basis. The tendency toward stagnation will inevitably dominate.

The Militarization of the National Economy Seriously Undermines the Social Productive Force

The militarization of the national economy runs into a blind alley that imperialist economic development must ultimately follow. It is an inevitable result of the development of the inherent contradictions of capitalism and is also a concrete manifestation of the increasingly decaying nature of imperialism.

To reduce the contradiction between the growth of capitalist productive forces and inadequate effective demand for the laboring masses and to avoid economic crises and redivide the world to obtain high monopoly profits, imperialism madly expands rearmament to prepare for wars. An increasing amount of the national income is used to support a large army, make weapons, support war-related research, and engage in imperialist aggressive wars.

The militarization of the national economy in the imperialist countries is first expressed in the increase of military expenditures. After the Second World War, the share of military defense expenditures in the United States budget steadily increased. From 1946 to 1970, direct United States military expenditures totaled 1,100 billion dollars, averaging 45 billion dollars a year.

In the 1972-73 fiscal year, direct military expenditures totaled

78.3 billion dollars. With 11.7 billion dollars as subsidies for veterans and 3.2 billion dollars for the space program, the three items added up to 93.2 billion dollars. It was also manifested in the increasing shares of industrial production and scientific research in armament industries and military scientific research. A large amount of the labor force was transferred from the production sphere of social wealth to armament industries and military scientific research fields. In 1967-68, the level of employment in United States armament production in several sectors and its ratio to the total labor force were: 126,900 in electronic equipment, or 33.8 percent; 256,900 in radio equipment, television sets, and telecommunications tools, or 38.6 percent; and 615,900 in aircraft and accessories, or 72.4 percent. Of the total United States scientific and technical manpower, two-thirds is related to armament and space research. In the United States labor force of 77 million (excluding armed forces), about 20 percent depends on armament orders from the Defense Department.

The general militarization of the national economy in the imperialist countries led to serious unfavorable consequences. In recent years, the United States has spent about 100 billion dollars on armament and aggression. The products are either used to murder people in the battlefield and destroy social wealth or, if stored away, soon become scrap. They may become "obsolete" before even leaving the plant when new weapons are invented. The militarization of the national economy has brought about strange results: the inflationary expansion of the armament industry and the deflationary contraction of civilian industries. In the past twenty years, the production of guided missiles, aircrafts, and space vehicles in the aeronautics and space industries in the United States has increased its value by six times. On the other hand, the development of civilian industries has been slow. Some industries have had to reduce production. Take the textile industry as an example. The output in 1970 was only 88 percent that of 1950. The policy of aggression and wars pursued by imperialism and the militarization of the national economy lead to an immense waste of manpower, goods, and wealth and to great destruction of social wealth. This is a notable feature of the decaying nature of imperialism.

The Bourgeoisie Increasingly Becomes a Stratum That Thrives Solely on Interest

The parasitic and decaying nature of imperialism is further manifested by the bourgeoisie's increasingly becoming a stratum that thrives solely on interest. This so-called stratum that thrives on interest refers to those who have lost all connection with the production process and "live on interest." The bourgeoisie has never been engaged in production labor and has led an extravagant life by exploiting the worker. In the stage of imperialism, the parasitic nature of the bourgeoisie develops further. Capitalist enterprises are wholly managed by specialized managerial personnel. The bourgeoisie, especially the monopoly bourgeoisie, is completely divorced from the production process and lives a parasitic life solely on income from stocks and shares. Lenin pointed out long ago, 'Imperialism is simply a great concentration of money capital in a few countries," "and thus the stratum of people who live on interest and do not work increases rapidly." (2) For example, the income from dividends and individual interest in the United States in 1950 totaled 19.5 billion dollars. In 1963, it reached 50.3 billion dollars, an increase of 157 percent. The national income increased by only 102 percent in the same period. In 1970, the income from dividends and individual interest in the United States reached 89.7 billion dollars. The United States monopoly bosses lead extravagant lives with the income from exploitation. Some bosses of financial groups not only build villas, golf courses, and hunting grounds, using a lot of land for their own pleasure, but also show off their riches to each other. In 1964, one big United States monopoly capitalist named Ford spent half a million dollars for a party to celebrate his daughter's birthday.

Not too long afterward, another big monopoly capitalist named Mellon spent a million dollars on a party to introduce his daughter to "society" to impress Ford. This incident fully exposed the parasitic nature of the monopoly bourgeoisie.

Another feature of imperialism is a rapid increase in capital export. With the increase in capital export, a few rich countries can become interest-earning countries that specialize in exploiting the people of colonies and satellite countries, being parasites on many economically underdeveloped countries. According to statistics, from 1950 to 1970 the interest from direct private United States investment reached 88.77 billion dollars, 14 percent higher than the total amount of direct private foreign investment up to the end of 1970. Direct United States investment in Latin America was 3 billion dollars in 1946 and increased to 11.7 billion dollars in 1969. But in these twenty- four years, interest derived from direct investment in Latin American countries which was paid to the United States alone amounted to 23.49 billion dollars, much higher than the net amount of direct United States investment.

United States interest derived from overseas is largely remitted annually to the United States to be spent by a handful of monopoly bourgeoisie. In the 1960-1970 period, remitted interest reached 43.4 billion dollars. During this period, unremitted interest amounting to 19 billion dollars was used for reinvestment to increase foreign exploitation. Thus, with United States imperialism's annual increase in foreign investment and interest, its parasitic nature also increased yearly.

All this shows that capital export is a solid foundation for imperialism's oppression and exploitation of the majority of nations and countries and a solid foundation for the parasitic capitalism of a few rich countries.

Th e Appearance of Worker- Elites Is Another Manifestation of the Parasitic Nature of Capitalism

The parasitic nature of imperialism is inevitably reflected in the labor movement. The formation of worker-elites and the appearance of revisionism are reflections of the parasitic nature of imperialism in the labor movement. Lenin pointed out:

'Interest-earning countries are parasitic and decaying capitalist countries. This condition cannot but have effects on all social and political conditions of these countries, especially on two basic factions in the labor movement." (3) The monopoly bourgeoisie plunders and exploits the proletariat of colonies, satellite countries, and their own countries to obtain large amounts of high monopoly profits. To suppress opposition from the toiling masses, they use a small part of the huge monopoly profits to bribe a number of scabs to become agents of the monopoly bourgeoisie. These are worker-elites who get high salaries and live like the bourgeoisie, serving the monopoly bourgeois class. They mingle with the workers and specialize in selling out the interests of the working class and subverting worker movements. These worker-elites are loyal running dogs of the monopoly bourgeoisie of the imperialist countries.

High profits from monopoly capital is the economic basis of revisionism in the labor movement. Under imperialist conditions and with the appearance of the worker-elites, a revisionist theory and line to protect imperialist rule emerges. The worker- elites are bourgeois elements disguised as workers. Revisionism is a bourgeois class theory under the guise of Marxism.

The worker-elites and revisionists are the most treacherous hidden enemies in the labor movement, and they may be regarded as boils on the body. If these boils are not completely removed, imperialism will maintain its decaying condition for a longer period of time. But, just as Lenin pointed out, "The rapid and vicious development of opportunism does not assure its victory." (4) Lenin further pointed out, 'If the struggle against imperialism is not closely associated with the struggle against opportunism, then it is just so many empty words." (5)

Toward Total Political Reaction and the Steady Increase in the Severity of Social Crises

In the stage of capitalist free competition, the bourgeoisie still uses "democracy," "freedom," "equality," and "universal love" as guises to conceal the truth of bourgeois dictatorship.

In the stage of imperialism, these thin "veils" are steadily trimmed down. Whoever opposes oppression and exploitation will be cruelly suppressed. Lenin pointed out: "The political superstructure of this new economic order, namely, monopoly capitalism (imperialism is monopoly capitalism), is transformed from democracy to political reaction. Free competition requires democracy,but monopoly requires political reaction." (6)

In the United States, not only people who oppose violence were suppressed, but people who championed nonviolence have also been slaughtered. In 1968, a black American minister named Martin Luther King was murdered by the United States imperialists because he opposed racial discrimination and fought for civil rights. In line with total political reaction, imperialism has also degenerated in its ideology and culture. In imperialist countries, publications and movies devoted to violence and sex have flooded the market. In California, there have been thirty companies specializing in making sex movies. In the capitalist world, strange clothing, modern dances, and "Beatles" music bands have been common, and exhibitions of "impressionist" art painted by monkeys have been much in vogue. International contests of women "crying" and crawling races for babies under a year old are reported to have taken place. The culture and art under imperialism have been rotten to the core. Criminal activities such as theft and robbery and gangsterism and drug abuse have reached crisis proportions.

Facing this rotten society, many youths perceive a spiritual void, feeling that life is empty and meaningless and without a future. Some United States historians think that the United States "faces a situation in which the people have lost faith in their ideals, system, and future" and "are plagued by numerous crises." Some are even more blunt: "Our crises, which are spiritual in nature, can be traced to the obvious failure of our self- inflating capitalist social system" (Newsweek, July 6, 1970). Amidst the profound contradictions of imperialism, a few progressive elements gradually wake up to accept Marxism and reestablish the Marxist party and organization, unite the masses, and engage in resolute struggle against the imperialist system.

The parasitic and decaying nature of imperialism which results from the basic characteristic of imperialism, namely, monopoly, reveals that imperialism is merely a paper tiger.

It looks fierce, but in fact it does not have much strength. The masses are the ones with real power, not imperialism or reactionaries. Just as Chairman Mao pointed out, "From a strategic viewpoint, or a long-run viewpoint, or looking at their substance, we must in effect treat imperialism and all reactionaries as paper tigers." (7)

Imperialism Is Dying Capitalism

The Intensification of the Contradiction between the Proletariat and the Bourgeoisie within the Imperialist Countries

Stalin said: "Lenin called imperialism 'dying capitalism.' Why? Because imperialism carries the contradictions of capitalism to their end. What follows is the beginning of revolution." (8) When capitalism develops into the monopoly stage, the basic contradictions between the proletariat and the bourgeoisie and the capitalist nature of society have not changed. However, in the imperialist stage, monopoly has not only pushed social production to a larger scale but has also brought about even more concentration of the private ownership of the means of production. The development of the basic contradictions of capitalism intensifies all external and internal contradictions of imperialism. Chairman Mao pointed out, "The intensification of the contradiction between the two classes (the proletariat and the bourgeoisie), the development of contradictions between monopoly and competitive capital, the intensification of contradictions between the suzerain and the colonies, and the acute manifestation of contradictions among imperialist countries due to their uneven development lead to a special stage of capitalism, namely, imperialism." (9) Because of the serious intensification of all external and internal contradictions in imperialist countries, imperialism becomes dying capitalism, and the eve of proletarian socialist revolution draws near.

To pursue high monopoly profits, the monopoly bourgeoisie doubles its efforts to exploit and plunder the workers and push millions of laboring masses to the brink of starvation. The monopoly bourgeoisie devises various intensive labor systems, raises labor intensity, worsens labor conditions, and indiscriminately and incessantly increases its exploitation of the workers. The bourgeoisie also consciously relies on inflation to reduce real wages and lower purchasing power. For example, in the 1963-1970 period, prices and the cost of living increased yearly in major capitalist countries because of inflation. In this period, the United States' cost of living increased 26.8 percent. In Britain, it increased 35.3 percent; in France, 30.9 percent; in West Germany, 20.6 percent; and in Japan, 44.4 percent. Wages, however, did not increase sufficiently to offset inflation and the increasing cost of living. The livelihood of the laboring people worsened further. Through the government, monopoly capital plundered the laboring masses even more with excessive taxation. In the 1940-1970period, tax revenue in the United States increased by sixteen times, from 16.5 billion dollars in 1940 (20 percent of the national income) to 278 billion dollars in 1970 (35 percent of the national income). Heavy taxation weighed down the laboring people, choking them breathless.

To protect its economic interests, monopoly capital inevitably resorts to fascist dictatorship to intensify the suppression of the workers through the state machinery. Overall political reaction is a natural political reflection of a monopoly capitalist economy. To implement fascist dictatorship and to suppress the people, imperialism expands the reactionary government machinery to a horrifying extent. Take the United States for example, where one out of every twenty people is an employee of the reactionary state machinery.

The ruthless economic exploitation and bloodthirsty political suppression of the proletariat by the monopoly bourgeoisie intensify the contradiction between the proletariat and the bourgeoisie. The heavier the oppression, the stronger the resistance. The daily awakening of millions of members of the proletariat and the laboring masses continuously wages revolutionary struggle against the capitalist system.

Since the Second World War, especially in recent years, strong and massive worker movements have come into existence. The struggle against imperialism is intensifying. According to obviously deflated official United States figures, in 1970 United States workers were on strike 5,600 times and 3.3 million workers participated. In 1971, both a nationwide strike involving 500,000 telephone workers and a strike involving 160,000 railway workers occurred. In the strikes, the workers chanted the combat slogan of "oppose (aggressive) wars, oppose poverty, oppose oppression," and they increasingly combined economic struggle with political struggle. According to official data from Britain (also obviously deflated), in 1970 there were 3,888 strikes with 1.65 million workers participating. In 1971, 13.5 million workdays were lost in connection with strikes in Britain. The revolutionary struggles of the Japanese working class have also gathered strength. According to official Japanese statistics, the number of so-called "labor-capital disputes" (actually struggles of the worker against the capitalist) increased from 1,345 in 1955 to 5,283 in 1969, an increase of 2.9 times. In the same period, the number participating increased from 3.748 million to 14.483 million, an increase of about three times.

The mushrooming development of worker movements is a revolt by a vital organ of imperialism. It promotes the further deterioration of capitalist economic and political crises and incessantly deals serious blows to the rule of monopoly capital. The fate of imperialism is increasingly precarious.

The Contradiction between Imperialism and the Oppressed Nations Widens

"Colonies were seized with gunpowder and swords." (10) After it has seized colonies and semicolonies with force, imperialism ruthlessly exploits and enslaves these areas and nations.

To exercise political control, it buttresses puppets, stations armed forces, and establishes military bases. To facilitate economic exploitation, it forcibly opens trading ports, controls customs and external trade, monopolizes money and finance, and forcibly seizes the rights to mine, operate factories, and navigate on inland waterways. To obtain high monopoly profits, the imperialist country ruthlessly exploits and oppresses the people of the colonies and semicolonies. The contradictions between imperialism and the oppressed nations are aggravated to an unprecedented degree. Imperialism controls the economic pulse of the colonies and semicolonies and colludes with local feudal power and comprador capital to restrict the development of their national economies. Imperialism also resorts to various measures to force the national economies of the colonies and semicolonies to be "simplified," that is, to produce only a few commodities required by foreign monopoly organizations, and thus cause their economic development to be lopsided and abnormal. As a result, the economies of these areas cannot be independent or self-sufficient, but can only rely on imperialism.

Since the Second World War, new upsurges have been appearing continuously in the national liberation movements of Asia, Africa, and Latin America. Many countries and areas have freed themselves from the fetters of imperialism and colonialism and have started on their independent roads. However, imperialism will never automatically retreat from the large areas of Asia, Africa, and Latin America. In addition to their usual colonial measures, they have increasingly resorted to neocolonial measures and have vainly attempted, under the guise of economic "aid," to further their vicious scheme of controlling these newly emerging independent countries. Through "aid," the capitalists have sought to dump their surplus goods and have used "aid" as a means of selling commodities. Through "aid," they have sought to control the economic policy of the recipient countries and control the development of these national economies. When some countries have refused to buy this imperialist trick, the imperialists have resorted to aggression and subversion and have gathered reactionary forces to instigate coups d'etat and overthrow progressive governments that have opposed imperialism and insisted on national independence.

The cruel plunder and bloodstained enslavement have widened and intensified the contradictions between the imperialists and the oppressed nations and peoples. From the day when the imperialist bandits set their feet on the sacred land of Asia, Africa, and Latin America, the oppressed nations and people who dearly treasure their freedom and independence have taken up stones, bows and arrows, spears, and artilleries to deal blows to imperialism. The heavier the exploitation and the tighter the oppression by imperialism, the more intense has become the resistance struggle of the oppressed nations and peoples. After the October Revolution, the national liberation movement ushered in a new historical era, constituting part of the proletarian socialist world revolution. The national liberation movements and the proletarian revolutionary movements in the imperialist countries are interrelated and mutually supporting. The colonies and semicolonies, once the reserve army of imperialism, have now become the reserve army of the proletarian world revolution. Just as Chairman Mao pointed out, "The revolutionary storm which has swept over Asia, Africa, and Latin America will surely deal a decisive and demolishing blow to the whole old world." (11)

The Intensification of Contradiction s among Imperialist Countries

Imperialism's struggle to divide the world economically and territorially has intensified the contradictions among the imperialist countries. Their struggles for hegemony and territory and their mutual fighting and massacring will really help the oppressed and exploited nations rise up to revolt.

The increasingly uneven economic and political development among capitalist countries in the imperialist stage further intensifies the contradictions among the imperialist countries.

Lenin pointed out, "Uneven economic and political development is the absolute law of capitalism." (12) In the capitalist world, some countries develop faster, and others slower. Some countries even advance by leaps and bounds in certain periods of time. The uneven economic development among the capitalist countries inevitably leads to uneven political development. In other words, uneven economic development must inevitably lead to changes in the relative strength of the imperialist countries.

The law of uneven economic and political development has played a role in the whole history of capitalism. However, in the imperialist period, this uneven development of capitalism intensifies. In the second half of the nineteenth century, England, an old capitalist country, seized a great number of colonies and assumed a monopoly position in the world. Her relatively easy and complacent position of manipulating high profits from her territories all over the world lulled her into stagnation in technology and production. Meanwhile, armed with new technology, the capitalist countries which arose later, especially the United States and Germany, accelerated their development. In the 1880s, the United States had already caught up with England and had taken the lead in world industrial production, and by the early twentieth century, Germany had also surpassed England, assuming second place in world industrial production. The shift in the relative positions of economic strength had brought about a relative shift in political power. Following the shift of the balance of power, the countries began to struggle to redivide their spheres of influence and colonies.

Since the Second World War, the law of uneven economic and political development among imperialist countries has continued to play a role. Its characteristics have been: the decline of the United States, the continued decline of England, the rapid ascension of West Germany and Japan, and the substantial gains of Italy and France. In the twenty years from 1949 to 1969, the annual average growth rates in the national product of these countries were: the United States — 3.9 percent in the first ten years and 4.3 percent in the second ten years; England — 2.5 percent in the first ten years and 3 percent in the second ten years; West Germany — 7.4 percent in the first ten years and 5.2 percent in the second ten years; France — 4.5 percent in the first ten years and 5.9 percent in the second ten years;

Italy — 6.1 percent in the first ten years and 5.6 percent in the second ten years; Japan — more than 10 percent for the whole period. New and uneven conditions appeared in their relative strength in terms of industrial production, capital and commodity exports, and international financial positions. The intensification of uneven economic and political development among the imperialist countries inevitably intensified the struggles among them for markets and supply bases for raw materials and for outlets for capital exports.

The operation of the law of uneven economic and political development inevitably led to wars and slaughter among the im - perialist countries, thus revealing their weak links. These then became favorable conditions for the proletariat and the revolutionary peoples to bury imperialism. In his study of the laws of imperialist development, Lenin arrived at an important conclusion: Because of their uneven economic and political development, the imperialist battlefront will be smashed at its weakest link, and socialist revolution will first triumph in one or several countries. Lenin not only created a revolutionary theory for our achievement of victory, he also set a brilliant example of how to carry out revolution. In the First World War, Russia was the focal point of all contradictions in imperialism at that time and was also the weakest link in the imperialist chain. Lenin seized this link and led the Russian proletariat to launch the great socialist October Revolution, overthrow the Russian bourgeois dictatorship with revolutionary violence, establish the world's first socialist country under proletarian dictatorship, and usher in a new era in human history. After the Second World War, the great victory of the national revolutions in China and other countries of Asia and Europe further confirmed the accuracy of Lenin's scientific theory.

The outbreak of the two world wars, the victorious march of the proletarian socialist revolutions, and the upsurge of national liberation movements further aggravated imperialism's political, economic, and social crises.

Although immense changes have occurred in the world, the imperialist period is not yet over. Chairman Mao often teaches us: We are still in the period of imperialism and proletarian revolution. Lenin's scientific analysis of imperialism based on the fundamental principles of Marxism is entirely correct. The basic principle of Leninism is not outdated; today it still remains the theoretical basis of our thought.

The life of imperialism will not be long. It is parasitic and dying capitalism on the eve of proletarian socialist revolution.

But, it will never retreat from the historical stage of its own free will. The nature of imperialism determines that the closer it draws to the end of its life, the more desperately it will struggle for survival. We must realize that imperialism is basically weak, a paper tiger. We must cultivate a bold spirit, daring to struggle and being good at struggle. And we must unite the revolutionary peoples of the world to carry the struggle against imperialism to the end. "Make trouble, fail, make trouble again, fail again until doom — this is the logic used by imperialism and all reactionary groups of the world to deal with the people's uprisings. They will never deviate from this logic." (13) Making trouble is an expression of the desperate struggle of imperialism; to be doomed to failure until its elimination is the inevitable destiny of imperialist development. No one can change this law of history.

Major Study References

Lenin, Imperialism, the Highest Stage of Capitalism, chaps. 7-10.

Lenin, 'Imperialism and the Split in the Socialist Movement." Chairman Mao, "Talk with American Correspondent Anna Louise Strong."

Review Problems

1. Why do we say that imperialism and all reactionaries are paper tigers?

2. Why do we say that imperialism is the eve of proletarian socialist revolution?

Notes

1) Imperialism, the Highest Stage of Capitalism, Selected Works of Lenin, Vol. 2, Jen-min ch'u-pan-she, 1972, p. 842.

2) Ibid., p. 818.

3) Ibid., p. 820.

4) Ibid., p. 843.

5) Ibid.

6) "On the Ridicule of Marxism and 'Imperialist Economism,'" Complete Works of Lenin, Vol. 23, p. 34.

7) Notes on "Talk with American Correspondent Anna Louise Strong," Selected Works of Mao Tse-tung, Vol. 4, Jen- min ch'u-pan-she, 1968, p. 1088.

8) "On the Basis of Leninism," Complete Works of Stalin, Vol. 6, p. 65.

9) M On Contradiction," S elected Works of Mao Tse-tung, Vol. 1, Jen-min ch'u-pan-she, 1968, p. 289.

10) "Socialism and War," Selected Works of Lenin, Vol. 2, Jen-min ch'u-pan-she, 1972, p. 672.

11) Chairman Mao, "A Congratulatory Telegram to the Fifth Congress of the Labor Party of Albania," quoted in Jen-min jih-pao [People's Daily], November 4, 1966.

12) "On the Slogan of European Alliance," Complete Works of Lenin, Vol. 21, p. 321.

13) "Cast Away Illusions and Prepare for Struggle," Selected Works of Mao Tse-tung, Vol. 4, Jen-min ch'u-pan-she, 1968, p. 1375.

11. Soviet Revisionist Social Imperialism Joins the Ranks of World Imperialism

Social Imperialism Is Socialism in Name but Imperialism in Substance

In the process of imperialism's gradual extinction, there emerged, in the mid-twentieth century, Soviet social imperialism. Under the leadership of Lenin and Stalin, Russia was once a great socialist country. But after Stalin passed away, the renegade clique of Khrushchev and Brezhnev launched a counterrevolutionary coup, seized Party and government power, restored capitalism in a big way, and transformed the Soviet Union into a social imperialist country.

During the First World War, Lenin denounced Kautsky, the head of the German Social Democratic Party at that time, as being a '"social imperialist,' that is, one who is nominally a socialist, but actually an imperialist." (1) The renegade clique of Brezhnev, like Kautsky, is also social imperialist. The only difference is that it not only peddles revisionism, but also defends imperialism. What is more, it controls state power, and has transformed a great country created by Lenin himself into a social imperialist country. Social imperialism is imperialism with a "socialist" label. The fact that it emerged in the Soviet Union, Lenin's homeland and once a great socialist country, makes it more deceptive and dangerous. It is a very vicious imperialism indeed.

State Monopoly Capitalism Is the Main Economic Basis of Social Imperialism

The Forma t ion of the Soviet Union's State Monopoly Capitalism

Whether it is capital imperialism or social imperialism, they are identical in their basic economic characteristics. Their main economic basis is monopoly capitalism. But, in capital imperialist countries, there are two forms of monopoly capitalist economy, namely, private and state monopoly capitalism In social imperialist countries, monopoly capitalism always takes the form of state monopoly capitalism. State monopoly capitalism is the main economic basis of social imperialism. This difference between social and capital imperialism is determined by the different historical conditions under which monopoly capital was created.

The monopoly capital of the capital imperialist countries was formed gradually in the process of acute competition in the private capitalist economy through capital accumulation and concentration. There, private monopoly capitalism appeared first and existed on a large scale. Only after private monopoly capitalism had developed to a certain extent and when monopoly capital and state power had combined with the state machinery to serve monopoly capital did state monopoly capitalism arise. State monopoly capitalism in the social imperialist country appeared when the people in power taking the capitalist road usurped the Party and government power in the socialist country and, in the process, transformed the socialist economy to restore capitalism.

After the Soviet renegade clique usurped the Party and government power in the Soviet Union, the Russian bourgeois privileged stratum greatly expanded its own political and economic power, assuming a dominant position in the Party, government, military, and economic and cultural spheres and forming a bureaucratic monopoly bourgeoisie which controls the whole state machinery and social wealth. This new bureaucratic monopoly bourgeoisie used the state power under its control to transform socialist ownership into ownership by those taking the capitalist road and to transform the socialist economy into a capitalist economy and a state monopoly capitalist economy.

The nature of a society's economy cannot be determined by its label, but by the ownership of the means of production. In other words, it must be determined by who owns the means of production, who allocates it, and whom it serves. After the renegade clique of Khrushchev and Brezhnev usurped Party and government power in the Soviet Union, it exercised total control over political and economic power and pursued a thoroughly revisionist line in the economic sphere. It extolled the "ruble as a measure of labor merit" and "the ability to earn a profit as the best criterion for evaluating Communist

Party members in charge of operations and management." Under the support of the Soviet revisionist renegade clique, Liberman, an economist of revisionism, proposed a scheme of state enterprise management that relied on profit and material incentives, and the "experiment" was widely disseminated. Since Brezhnev succeeded Khrushchev, the "new economic system" has been instituted nationwide. The profit principle of capitalism has been legally affirmed to strengthen the exploitation of the laboring people by the bureaucratic monopolist oligarchy. With these "transformations," the means of production which formerly belonged to the people of the Soviet Union are now owned by and at the service of the new bureaucratic monopoly bourgeoisie. The worker and peasant of the Soviet Union have been deprived of their means of production and reduced once more to hired laborers. Although the Soviet Union may still carry the socialist label, the original socialist ownership system has in fact been transformed into an ownership system of the bureaucratic monopoly bourgeoisie.

In socialist society, the state-ope rated economy based on socialist state ownership is a leading element in the national economy. Once the revisionist renegade clique usurps the leadership of the socialist economy, it is naturally transformed into a state monopoly capitalist economy. This is because the more productive forces the new bureaucratic monopoly bourgeoisie puts under state ownership representing its interests, the more it can control the whole society's wealth in the name of the "state." This way, it not only can continue using the state label to deceive the laboring people, but through state capitalism can also tightly control the national economy. Therefore, the outstanding characteristic of the Soviet Union's capitalist economy is that state monopoly capitalism controls and commands everything. This situation is rare in the capital imperialist country. In the capital imperialist country, although state monopoly capitalism has undergone sizable development, it has not yet reached the state which prevails in the Soviet Union. Because of exploitation and oppression, the Soviet working class, especially the mass of laboring people, has suffered heavily. Lenin once pointed out: "Under private ownership of the means of production, more monopolization and nationalization will inevitably lead to greater exploitation and oppression of the laboring masses and to greater difficulties in staging revolts. Similarly, any strengthening of the reactionary military dictatorship will inevitably result in raising the capitalist profits exploited from other classes and in inflicting decades of suffering on the working class who will have to pay the capitalists for the billions of dollars which the military dictatorship has borrowed." (2)

As we read this passage by Lenin, it sounds like an accurate economic analysis of Soviet state capitalism. Nekarsov, a well-known Russian poet, denounced in grief and anger the black rule of the old czar, "In Russia, who can be happy or free?" Today in Russia, the children of the heroes of the October Revolution are suffering multiple hardship with no joy or freedom to speak of. But the bureaucratic monopoly bourgeoisie headed by Brezhnev plunder the state treasury,,lead extravagant lives, exercise cruel and arbitrary rule, and suck the blood and sweat of the people of the Soviet Union at will. The bureaucratic monopoly bourgeoisie headed by Brezhnev is the class basis of social imperialism and a "personification" of state capitalism.

The Trust Is the Basic Form of the Monopoly Organization of Soviet Revisionism

An important form of organization in the state capitalism of Soviet revisionism is the "trust." The ways in which trusts are established differ from the monopoly organization of capitalist countries. They are formed by merging the big enterprises with many medium and small enterprises through the use of state coercion.

The trust as a form of monopoly organization developed rapidly in the Soviet Union. In 1961, there were only 2 such trusts. Ten years later, in June 1971, there were 1,400 such trusts with more than 14,000 enterprises and 7.7 million employees. Nearly one-third of the mining enterprises were trusts. At the "Twenty-fourth National Congress" of the Soviet Union, Brezhnev exclaimed, 'The policy to establish trusts and merged enterprises must be carried out more resolutely — in the future, they should become the basic economic accounting unit in social production." Following the order of the Soviet revisionist leadership group, since 1971 the trust system has extended its sphere of dominance to include all the Soviet Union's manufacturing sectors.

There are three basic types of Soviet revisionist trusts:

First, the absorbed enterprises 'lose their independence and status as legal persons." The trust becomes "the basic economic accounting unit of social production" and possesses all the rights over its subordinate enterprises.

Second, some absorbed enterprises lose their legal independence, while others "maintain relative independence."

Third, the absorbed enterprises are "still independent," but are administered by the trust.

Of the above three types of trusts, Soviet revisionism emphasized the development of the first type. It was modeled after that of Western monopoly capitalist enterprises and "used" their "organization system chart." Soviet revisionism publicized the trust as "embodying a compressed and dormant future structure of Russian industries" and as being a type of "special Russian consortium." The trust not only engages in production, but also deals with the supply of raw materials and the distribution of products. The difference between the trust and the Western monopoly capitalist enterprise is that the alliance between the Russian trust and state power is much closer. It is not only a basic economic accounting unit, it also carries out part of the functions originally exercised by the General Control Bureau or even the Ministry of Control with respect to planning, production, supply, and distribution. Large and regional trusts are "not only an integrated production unit but also an economic management organ." There are no middle organs between the various ministries in charge of economic control and the trusts. The managers of the trust, like the secretaries and deputy secretaries of government ministries, are listed as "leading members of the national economy" of Soviet revisionism. They are important members of the bureaucratic monopoly bourgeoisie headed by Brezhnev. Therefore, the trust is an entity that unifies the state organ and the monopoly organization and is an important form in the administrative system of state monopoly capitalism.

Apart from the fact that the trust is a monopoly organization, the state enterprise of Soviet revisionism has long been capitalistic. In the state enterprise of Soviet revisionism, the working masses have long been reduced from being the masters of the enterprise to slaves of the bureaucratic monopoly bourgeoisie.

The leaders of the enterprise are the agents of the leadership group of Soviet revisionism. According to the codes of the "Regulations of Socialist State Production Enterprises," the manager of the enterprise exercises the "power to recruit and dismiss personnel and makes decisions regarding rewards and punishment for the enterprise's personnel." He has the authority to determine the wages and bonuses of the staff and workers and to resell or rent the enterprise's means of production. In sum, even without the trust, the manager and the plant director are already rulers possessing all the power in state enterprises, and the broad masses of workers are already slaves of the bureaucratic monopoly bourgeoisie. Now, with the trust as a monopoly organization, the bureaucratic monopoly bourgeoisie can further strengthen its control over the pulse of the national economy in the Soviet Union. This new-style big bourgeoisie, using the state enterprises and trusts it controls and availing itself of the name of the state, has used taxation and surrendered profits to unrestrainedly plunder the fruits of the Russian worker's labor in order to support the extravagant lives of a few monopoly capitalists, suppress the Soviet people, launch aggression, and pursue its social imperialist policy.

While the renegade clique of Brezhnev was developing monopoly organizations in manufacturing and mining in a big way, various types of monopoly organizations were also developed in agriculture. They included: (1) the agricultural trust which is a trust organization of specialized state farms such as the poultry, livestock, and vegetable trusts; (2) the agricultural trust which is an organization of several state farms or collective farms or between state farms and collective farms; and (3) the agricultural-industrial complex, also called the agricultural- industrial joint enterprise which is a trust by which the agricultural enterprise directly operates processing plants for agricultural produce. Through these agricultural monopoly organizations, the bureaucratic monopoly bourgeoisie strengthened their control and plundered the broad Soviet countryside.

The "Shchekino Experiment" Was the Model of the Oppressive System Implemented by Soviet Revisionist Monopoly Enterprise

The neomonopoly capitalist bureaucrats, having put the national economy under their control and totally restored the capitalist hired-labor system, stepped up their exploitation and oppression of the broad masses. Since 1967, the so-called "Shchekino experiment" has amply confirmed the restoration of capitalism in the Soviet Union.

Shchekino was a chemical enterprise located near Moscow which had more than 7,000 employees and produced chemical fertilizers and other chemical products. In August 1967, tailored to the demands of the Soviet revisionist bureaucratic monopoly bourgeoisie, the enterprise began a so-called "economic experiment to strengthen the employees' concern for increasing production, raise labor productivity, and reduce the number of personnel." This "experiment" continuously increased the workers' labor intensity through the measures of concurrent jobs, combined categories of work, and expanded scopes of service and achieved the goal of reducing personnel and raising labor intensity. At the same time, it was decided to freeze the enterprise's total wage fund for several years, and the wage fund thus saved by personnel retrenchment was left largely to the discretion of a handful of the privileged class in the enterprise. Brezhnev boasted that the "experiment" was a perfect remuneration model, and it has since been disseminated throughout the Soviet Union.

The heart of the "Shchekino experiment" is to "reduce the labor force to increase labor productivity" in order to push the enterprise to "tap its potential." How was labor productivity increased? The "Shchekino experiment" proved that it could be achieved by increasing labor intensity. According to the statistics of June 1971, since the Shchekino chemical joint enterprise implemented this "experiment," more than 1,000 workers had been dismissed, or more than one-seventh of the total staff and workers. Of these, 68 workers, or 6 percent, were dismissed due to either greater mechanization or the consequent reduction in labor intensity; while more than 90 percent of the workers were dismissed because of an increase in labor intensity. Marx pointed out, "The crucial problem of the whole capitalist production system is: to increase uncompensated labor through such measures as prolonging the workday, increasing productivity, and consequently making labor power more intense." (3) In the imperialist stage, the extraction of unpaid labor from the worker by monopoly capital was increased by a hundred times. In capital imperialist countries, monopoly capital used so-called "scientific management methods" such as the 'Taylor system" to force the worker to increase labor intensity by a big margin in order to increase the extraction of surplus value. The "Shchekino experiment" promoted by the renegade clique of Soviet revisionism was a carbon copy of the 'Taylor system" which was strongly denounced by Lenin as a "blood- and sweat-sucking system." Its intent was to force one Russian to do several workers' jobs and maliciously extract more surplus labor and surplus value from him.

As of July 1971, the 121 enterprises which implemented the "Shchekino experiment" had already dismissed 65,000 people. At present, heavy unemployment has begun to emerge in the Soviet Union. This economic system of state monopoly capitalism of Soviet revisionism has already pushed the relationship between capital and hired labor to its limit. It has already met, and will continue to encounter, strong opposition from the Soviet working class and the broad masses of laboring people.

Soviet Revisionist "New International Relations" Is Another Name for Neocolonialism

Economic Unification Is a Major Measure of the Neocolonialism Launched by Soviet Revisionism

To pursue high monopoly profits, monopoly capital, while increasing exploitation of the people at home, inevitably expands externally. Through capital export and by adopting colonial policies, it plunders and enslaves the people of other countries. The monopoly capitalism of Soviet revisionism naturally is not satisfied with the exploitation of the Soviet workers and peasant masses and inevitably extends its paws to foreign countries. The first to be so affected are the "fraternal countries" of that "big socialist family."

The renegade clique of Brezhnev trapped some Eastern European countries and Mongolia into a so-called "big socialist family."

The nominal relations between Soviet revisionism and the "fraternal countries" of this big family are "new socialist international relations." Actually, it is a cat and mouse relationship between the imperialist suzerain and the colonies. The Soviet Union resorted to the most brutal and vicious means to tightly control these countries. Militarily, it stationed sizable armed forces in some countries in line with the "Warsaw Pact" and other bilateral agreements. It even openly mobilized several hundred thousand troops to invade Czechoslovakia. Politically, it bribed, sabotaged, and even used bayonets to set up puppet governments. Economically, it pushed the so-called "economic unification" through the "Council for Mutual Economic Aid" (COMECON). Some Eastern European countries and Mongolia are virtually under colonial rule and suffer shocking exploitation.

The intent of the "economic unification" promoted by the social imperialism of Soviet revisionism is to dissolve the national economic systems of COMECON members, create a monolithic, lopsided colonial economy, and "unify" the territories, populations, and resources of these countries with the social imperialism of Soviet revisionism. Soviet revisionism's "international division of labor" and "production specialization" are both subject to "economic unification," serving the purpose of realizing the above-mentioned "economic unification."

One of the means used by Soviet revisionism to enslave the "fraternal countries" in the name of "economic unification" is to destroy the fuel and raw material industries of the COMECON member countries and to achieve a high degree of monopoly by Soviet revisionism. According to statistics released by COMECON and official Soviet revisionist sources, in the 1966-1970pe- riod, the percentages of imported fuel and raw materials going from the Soviet revisionists to Bulgaria, Hungary, the German Democratic Republic, Poland, and Czechoslovakia were:

93 percent for petroleum, 61.9 percent for coal, 86.8 percent for iron ore, 97.5 percent for pig iron, and 64.3 percent for raw cotton. The high degree of monopoly by the Soviet revisionists in the supply of fuel and raw materials to the member countries determined the fate of these countries.

Another means used by Soviet revisionism to enslave the "fraternal countries" in the name of "economic unification" was to force the member countries to specialize in products required by the Soviet revisionists. For example, Poland was forced to develop the shipbuilding industry, Czechoslovakia to specialize in railway rolling stock, the German Democratic Republic to produce mining equipment, Bulgaria to produce vegetables and fruits, and Mongolia to specialize in the livestock industry to provide meat for the Soviet revisionists. This way, the "fraternal countries" were transformed into affiliated processing plants, orchards and vegetable gardens, and livestock ranches for Soviet revisionism.

To accelerate "economic unification" and more effectively control the member countries, Soviet revisionism set up a series of "supranational organizations" such as the "International Metallurgical Industry Cooperative Organization," the "International Chemical Engineering Industry Cooperative Organization," the "International Economic Cooperative Bank," and the 'International Investment Bank." These "supranational organizations" are actually international monopoly organizations controlled by the state monopoly capitalism of Soviet revisionism. Through them, the vital departments of the national economies of the member countries are controlled by Soviet revisionism.

When Soviet revisionism had its hands at the throats of the "fraternal countries," coercing them to lopsidedly develop their economies in conformity with Soviet needs, it could plunder them through trade using monopoly and colonial rules. According to Soviet revisionist magazines, in 1970 Soviet revisionism accounted for 80 percent of Mongolia's total foreign trade, more than 50 percent of Bulgaria's, about 40 percent of that of the German Democratic Republic's, and about one-third of Poland's, Hungary's, and Czechoslovakia's. Taking advantage of its dominant position, Soviet revisionism has cruelly exploited these countries by trading with them on terms unfavorable to them. The Soviet Union traded Mongolia one bicycle for four horses and one toy lamb for one live lamb. The Soviet import price for electric locomotives from Czechoslovakia was two-fifths lower than the import price of the same item from West Germany. But the export price of iron ore from the Soviet revisionists to Czechoslovakia was more than twice as high as that to West Germany. The atomic reactors sold by Soviet revisionism to some Eastern European countries were at a price four times higher than in the international market. A former member of the Planning Commission of the German Democratic Republic complained that the annual loss suffered by his country from trading with the Soviet Union amounted to 2 billion marks.

Like capital imperialism, the social imperialism of Soviet revisionism exported capital to some Eastern European countries and Mongolia calling it "aid." Up to early 1971, Soviet revisionism exported capital totaling 2.15 billion rubles as longterm "loans." Through capital export, not only were large sums of money extracted in the form of interest, but the direction of development in the recipient countries was also controlled. Moreover, availing themselves of this exporting, they dumped large quantities of unmarketable commodities and equipment at high prices to obtain high monopoly profits.

While exporting capital, the Soviet revisionists, taking advantage of their predominate position in "economic unification" and under the pretext of the increasing demands by member countries for Soviet exports of raw materials, compelled some countries to provide the funds and manpower for the construction of Soviet plants and the exploration of Soviet mines. They engaged in naked plundering. For example, in 1966 Czechoslovakia was forced to furnish 500 million rubles to the Soviet revisionists for the purpose of buying steel pipes and petroleum equipment to develop the Tuimen oilfield. In 1968, Czechoslovakia was again forced to furnish large quantities of trucks and large caliber piping to construct a pipeline for Siberian natural gas. Soviet revisionism even'drafted several tens of thousands of laborers from Bulgaria to do hard labor, thus directly exploiting their surplus labor.

Lenin once denounced the old czar as "treating his neighboring countries according to the principle of prerogative under serfdom." (4) The conduct of Soviet revisionism toward its neighboring countries today is even worse than that of the old czar. The so-called "international division of labor" and "production specialization" in the service of Soviet revisionist "economic unification" is a "division of labor" between the suzerain and its colonies like the one advocated by the old Japanese militarism under the slogan of "industrial Japan, agricultural China." The "big socialist family" of Soviet revisionism is merely a different name for an imperialist sphere of influence like the "new European order" of Hitler's Germany and Japanese militarism's "East Asian Great Co-Prosperity Sphere." (4)

Carrying out a Colonial Expansion Policy in Asia, Africa, and Latin America under the Name of "Aid"

Because Soviet revisionism has transformed into social imperialism, it must also be subject to the laws governing imperialism. It naturally is not satisfied with colonial rule within the "big socialist family," but inevitably tries to monopolize more of the world's markets for its commodities, raw materials, and investment. Asia, Africa, and Latin America, with abundant resources and backward economies, have been the natural objects of Soviet revisionist colonial expansion.

The renegade clique of Soviet revisionism says it offers "aid" to Asia, Africa, and Latin America. But in fact, under the guise of "aid," it attempts in every way to bring some countries of these regions into its own sphere of influence and to struggle with United States imperialism to win over the third countries.

"Soviet aid" is a trojan horse which breaks its way into the "aid" recipient countries on all sides, carrying harsh political and economic conditions. It consists mainly of "military aid," namely, the sale of outdated military hardware. By this means, it controls and interferes with the "aid" recipient countries militarily, politically, and economically. Soviet revisionism annually gives one billion rubles in aid to regions in Asia, Africa, and Latin America: 30 percent as "economic aid" and 70 percent as "military aid." The key areas are the Middle East and the Persian Gulf area; next in line is the South Asian subcontinent. Because the Middle East and the Persian Gulf areas possess immense strategic value and are rich in oil, Soviet revisionism tries very hard in many countries in these areas to establish naval and air bases, control the prospecting, extracting, refining, and transportation of oil, and monopolize the purchase of oil through "Soviet aid." The South Asian subcontinent possesses not only important strategic value but also abundant natural and human resources. Soviet revisionism has plundered the resources of these areas and interfered with their politics (through exports of military hardware and capital at unfavorable terms of trade) while waiting for favorable opportunities to establish military bases.

In the South Asian subcontinent, India has received the largest share of "Soviet aid." Her economic pulse has been in the hands of Soviet revisionism. As of the end of 1970, the percentages of Indian industrial production coming from enterprises receiving Soviet "aid" were as follows: 30 percent of its steel output, 60 percent of its oil refining capacity, 85 percent of its heavy machines, 20 percent of its electricity output, 30 percent of its oil products, and 60 percent of its electricity-generating equipment. In the "aid assisted" projects, engineering designs were monopolized and totally controlled during the construction phase by Soviet revisionism. Even in operation, it was still impossible for India to be independent of the control of Soviet revision · ism. For the maintenance of equipment and the supply of parts and important materials, it had to rely on the Soviet revisionists. In addition, Soviet revisionism further controlled India's production by demanding that "Soviet aid" be repaid in kind.

Some of India's leather shoe factories, garment factories, dye factories, leather factories, and light bulb factories were set up to meet the Soviet Union's demand. The output of these plants was not for India's consumption, but for export to the Soviet Union to repay debts. It was in these ways that Soviet revisionism sought to take advantage of India's raw materials and cheap labor and turn India into its affiliated processing plant under the guise of "aid." The Indian press exclaimed, 'India is an egg that sits snugly in the Russian basket."

The renegade clique of Soviet revisionism boasts that only by relying on Soviet "aid" and entering into "international division of labor" "can the developing countries smoothly attain real political and economic independence and be capable of resisting imperialist power." This is indeed the greatest lie ever heard. Even Soviet revisionism had to admit that the division of labor between her and the developing countries was "strongly affected by the preexisting division of labor." Its characteristic is "the exchange of industrial products, especially machinery for raw materials, tropical produce and fuel." Over 95 percent of the Soviet revisionists' imports of rubber and 92 percent of their imports of cotton come from Asia, Africa, and Latin America. The Soviet revisionists trade their outdated machinery for oil from the Middle East, copper from Chile, tin from Bolivia, meat from East Africa, and uranium from Somalia. Is it not true that this pattern of "international division of labor" between the "industrial Soviet Union" and "agricultural Asia, Africa, and Latin America" is typical of the division of labor between a suzerain and its colonies?

The renegade clique of Soviet revisionism boasts that the interest on its loans, 2.5 percent per annum, is much lower than that charged by the capital imperialist countries and that the loans are "selfless aid." In fact, Soviet revisionist loans are a disguised form of usury. The usurious interest rate was concealed in the high prices charged for goods supplied. The Soviet loans extended to the countries of Asia, Africa, and Latin America had to be used for purchasing Soviet goods, consisting primarily of outdated weapons, old equipment, and unmarketable commodities. Not only were the products poor in quality and backward in technology, but they were also higher in price, some 20 percent, 30 percent, or even 100 percent higher than the prices on the international market. In addition, the Soviet revisionist social imperialists often pressed the debtor countries for payment, compelling them to supply the Soviet Union with certain raw materials. It was reported that the Soviet Union had signed an agreement with a Middle Eastern country demanding that the latter pay its debts to the former in oil from 1973 through 1980 at prices 20 percent below the international market price. What is labeled as "selfless aid" is in fact cruel exploitation.

Verbally, the renegade clique of the Soviet revisionists have promised "total support" for the revolutionary struggles of the peoples in Asia, Africa, and Latin America. In actuality, they have colluded with all the world's most reactionary powers to undermine the revolutionary struggles of these peoples and have pursued neocolonialism. They have supplied money and arms to help the reactionary groups of various countries massacre revolutionaries. They have dismembered Pakistan, supported the traitor clique of Lon Nol, engaged in sabotage in many countries of Asia, Africa, and Latin America, used all means to support the reactionary groups of various countries in Asia, Africa, and Latin America in order to extinguish the people's armed struggle, suppressed national liberation movements, and acted as the military police of the world.

Soviet Revisionist Imperialism Is the Eve of a Second October Revolution

The Extreme Parasitic and Decaying Nature of Soviet Revisionist Social Imperialism

Soviet revisionist social imperialism is monopoly capitalism. It cruelly exploits and oppresses its laboring people and ferociously plunders and enslaves the peoples of other countries, especially the broad masses in Asia, Africa, and Latin America.

It is even worse than capital imperialism. However, like all imperialism, Soviet revisionist state monopoly capitalism is just a paper tiger. Because all monopoly capitalism is necessarily at the same time both parasitic and decaying capitalism, it is moribund capitalism. Soviet revisionist state monopoly capitalism is no exception. Whether in its economic or political aspects, Soviet revisionist state monopoly capitalism reveals in every possible way its extreme parasitic and decaying nature. It will soon be sent to a museum by the people of the Soviet Union and the world.

The extreme decaying nature of Soviet revisionist social imperialism has been primarily revealed in its stagnating economic development. The production relation of Soviet revisionist state monopoly capitalism seriously hinders the development of social productive forces. When the Soviet Union was a socialist country, its industrial production in the ten-year period of 1929-1938 increased by leaps and bounds at an average annual rate of 17.4 percent. When the Soviet Union turned to social imperialism, the average annual growth rate of industrial production in the ten-year period of 1961-1970 declined sharply from 8.6 percent to 7.7 percent in 1971 and below 7 percent in 1972. Under the rule of the renegade clique of Khrushchev and Brezhnev, agricultural production in the Soviet Union was even worse. Serious agricultural crises erupted many times and large quantities of food had to be imported from the United States, Canada, and Australia.

Owing to industrial recession, declining agricultural output, dwindling livestock, and inflation, severe shortages of commodities and tight market supplies were reported. The livelihood of the laboring people was impoverished.

The extreme decaying nature of social imperialism has also been revealed in its frantic efforts at military expansion and war preparations. To pursue external aggression and expansion, the bureaucratic monopoly bourgeoisie represented by the Brezhnev renegade clique has inevitably followed the Hitler- type policy of "more guns and less butter" to militarize the national economy. According to estimates, the military expenditures of the Soviet revisionists were three to four times higher than those admitted by official sources. The average annual military expenditure since the 1970s has reached 80 billion dollars, or more than 30 percent of the state budget. To fight for naval supremacy, Soviet revisionism has greatly expanded its navy. Military expenditure on battleships has increased sharply year after year. According to estimates, the annual average expenditure in this area in the 1960s was 2 billion dollars. In 1970, it was increased to 3 billion dollars, or 0.9 billion dollars more than the United States spent on battleships in the same year. When large quantities of social wealth are not used to expand production to improve people's livelihood, but instead to expand armaments, prepare for wars, and pursue external aggression and expansion, it constitutes the most pronounced manifestation of social imperialism's decaying nature.

The extreme decaying nature of Soviet revisionist social imperialism has also been revealed in its total political reaction and serious deterioration of social life. Chairman Mao pointed out that "the present Soviet Union is a dictatorship of the bourgeoisie, a dictatorship of the big bourgeoisie, a German fascist- style dictatorship, a Hitler-type dictatorship." (5) Chairman Mao's analysis profoundly revealed the class nature and social origin of Soviet revisionist social imperialism, exposing its fascist nature and the lie of the Soviet revisionist renegade clique that the Soviet Union is "a country for all the people." When the Soviet revisionist renegade clique came to power, it tried very hard to strengthen its fascist dictatorship organ. It not only used the most modern scientific and technological means to equip its police and intelligence agencies to strengthen its suppression of the people, but also widely stationed secret agents in factories, farms, organizations, and associations to keep the masses in line. Today's Soviet Union is under a reign of white terror. Whoever dares to show discontent and resist the Brezhnev clique is watched, tailed, interrogated, or sent to a "mental asylum," concentration camp, or prison for the alleged crime of "slandering the Soviet Union or sabotaging the social order."

In addition to suppressing the people with naked violence, the renegade clique of Brezhnev has also used subtle measures to undermine the people by introducing the rotten culture, vulgar arts,and life-style from capital imperialist countries to poison the Soviet people. All the most ideologically backward, reactionary, and rotten things in the world have managed to find fertile soil in Soviet revisionist social imperialism.

Another manifestation of the extreme parasitic and decaying nature of Soviet revisionist social imperialism has been the much higher income of the bureaucratic monopoly bourgeoisie represented by the Brezhnev renegade clique than that received by the ordinary workers and peasants. The difference in income of more than 10 times, or even 100 times, was obtained through high wages, high bonuses, and various types of personal subsidies. This class has also taken advantage of its special economic and political privileges to serve its own selfish interests, engaging in corruption and leading extravagant, parasitic lives. Closely related to this bureaucratic monopoly bourgeoisie is a revisionist intellectual aristocracy. This revisionist intellectual aristocracy serves the bureaucratic monopoly bourgeoisie in the ideological sphere and leads an equally sensual, parasitic life. Sholokhov, an author known for his writing on the terror of war and bourgeois pacifism, became a billionaire. He owned not only a private car, but also a private airplane. His bank deposits were so huge that even he himself lost track of them.

In sum, a rotten atmosphere characteristic of a decaying social system has pervaded the economic, political, and cultural spheres of Soviet revisionist social imperialism. This social system, like the poisonous fungus growing on a pile of cow dung, is devoid of vitality.

A New Historical Period of Opposing United States Imperialism and Soviet Revisionism Has Already Begun

The bloodstained oppression and exploitation of the laboring people at home, the cruel colonial rule over countries in the,f big socialist family," and the aggressive expansion in various parts of the world have inevitably intensified the various contradictions which Soviet revisionist social imperialism faces at home and abroad.

Wherever there is oppression, there is resistance. The oppression and exploitation of the laboring people of the Soviet Union by the Soviet revisionist bureaucratic monopoly bourgeoisie inevitably meets the resistance of the Soviet laboring people.

The opposition of the Soviet people to the bureaucratic monopoly bourgeoisie takes many varied forms. The workers of many areas in the Soviet Union have resorted to slowdowns, negligence of duty, and strikes to show their discontent and opposition to the ruling clique of Soviet revisionism. In many places, the revolutionary masses have demonstrated many times, opposing the fascist dictatorship of Soviet revisionist authority. In various areas of the Soviet Union, people have frequently published underground materials, distributed leaflets to protest the reactionary rule of the Soviet revisionist renegade clique, and exposed the hidden secrets of the Soviet revisionist privileged class. The heroic children of the October Revolution will never submit to the reactionary rule of the new czar of Soviet revisionism. Under the dark rule of the old czar, Lenin confidently pointed out that 'the proletariat of Russia will spare nc sacrifice to free the whole of mankind from the humiliation of the czarist monarchy." (6) Today, the Soviet proletariat, peasants, and revolutionary intellectuals must answer Lenin's call and work for the overthrow of the new czar and the reestablishment of proletarian dictatorship.

Second, the contradiction between the countries and people being persecuted by Soviet revisionist neocolonialism and Soviet revisionist social imperialism has increasingly intensified.

The neocolonialist policy of "economic unification" pursued by Soviet revisionism and the enslavement and plundering of some Eastern European countries and Mongolia has furthered the development of antiplundering and antidomination struggles in these countries. The flagrant armed occupation of Czechoslovakia by the Soviet revisionists opened up the watchful eyes of some Eastern European countries and Mongolia and strengthened their struggle against Soviet revisionist social imperialism. Today, Eastern Europe is like a powder keg which may explode at some future date. The invasion of Prague by Soviet revisionist tanks did not demonstrate the might of the Soviet revisionist social imperialism; on the contrary, it was an omen of the beginning of the Soviet revisionist colonial empire's collapse.

Under the guise of "aid," Soviet revisionism frantically infiltrates, plunders, and invades the countries of Asia, Africa, and Latin America and sets itself in opposition to the people of Asia, Africa, and Latin America. The demonic paws of Soviet revisionist social imperialism have reached some countries in the Mediterranean and the Indian Ocean by establishing military bases, obtaining port privileges, and controlling and interfering with internal politics and foreign affairs. The Soviet fishing fleet cruises freely around the world, plundering and destroying fishing resources and encroaching on the territorial waters of other countries. The people of Asia, Africa, and Latin America are becoming more aware of the reactionary nature of Soviet revisionist social imperialism. They have solemnly pointed out that the Soviet revisionist renegade clique, which has betrayed "the world's revolutionary peoples," is a "neocolonialist" and "another public enemy of the people of the world." The countries and people who are subject to aggression, control, interference, and ill-treatment from Soviet revisionism and United States imperialism are uniting to victoriously launch an anti-imperialist and anticolonial struggle aimed particularly at the two nuclear superpowers, the United States and the Soviet Union.

Third, the frantic external aggression and expansion of Soviet revisionist social imperialism and its fight for commodity markets, supplies of raw materials, and investment outlets has intensified the contradictions among the imperialist countries to an unprecedented degree, especially those between Soviet revisionism and United States imperialism; the two nuclear superpowers wrestle for world hegemony.

Today, it is primarily the two nuclear superpowers, the United States and the Soviet Union, who are vying for world hegemony. The strategic point they are fighting for is in Europe because Europe is the heart of the capitalist world. The West always wants to push Soviet revisionism to expand eastward and divert this flood of disaster to China. But China is a tough piece of meat that has been resisting biting for many years. At present, Soviet revisionism, pursuing the strategy of feint attack, has stepped up its struggle in Europe. The Soviet revisionists have stationed two-thirds of their army and air force to the west of the Urals. The Soviet revisionist navy has expanded rapidly in the recent decade. In 1970, it dispatched more than 200 battleships to three oceans and eight seacoasts in a global exercise to show off its naval prowess and stepped up its expansion toward the Mediterranean and the Indian Ocean. The struggle for world hegemony between the United States and the Soviet Union is the source of world unrest. The struggle has encountered intense resistance from the Third World and created increasing displeasure in Japan and the West European countries. The expanding internal and external difficulties of the two powers put them in an increasingly unenviable and helpless situation.

Imperialism means aggression and war. Soviet revisionist social imperialism is stationing troops along China's borders, attempting to turn China into its colony. We must follow Chairman Mao's teachings to,T be prepared for war, be prepared for natural disasters, and do everything for the people" and to "dig deep caves, increase grain stocks, and never be aggressive" in order to strengthen preparations against aggressive wars and be on the alert for the outbreak of an imperialist world war, especially surprise attacks from Soviet revisionist social imperialism. We must resolutely, thoroughly, cleanly, and totally annihilate all enemies who dare to invade us.

Chairman Mao pointed out, 'The revolutionary people of the world will never forgive the numerous evil and scandalous deeds committed by Soviet revisionism in collusion with United States imperialism. The peoples of various countries are standing up. A new era opposing United States imperialism and Soviet revisionism is dawning." (7) In the struggle against the hegemony mentality and power politics, the Third World is awakening and growing. This is a big event in contemporary international relations. The characteristic of the contemporary international situation is perpetual chaos. '.'Strong winds fore- tell the coming storm." This is precisely the contemporary version of the world's basic contradictions which Lenin analyzed. All countries subject to aggression, sabotage, interference, control, and ill-treatment from imperialism have become increasingly united, forming a broad united front and strengthening their struggle against imperialism and new and old colonialism, especially against the hegemony mentality of the two superpowers, the United States and the Soviet Union. Countries must be independent, nations must be liberated, and people must make revolution. These are irresistible historical tides which will sweep away the United States and the Soviet Union.

On the eve of the victory of the Anti-Japanese War, Chairman Mao prophesied: "The world will advance and never regress. Naturally, however, we should be prepared to anticipate possible temporary, and even serious, historical detours. There are still very strong reactionary influences in many countries that are reluctant to see their own people and peoples of other countries achieve unity, progress, and liberation. Whoever ignores these factors will surely commit serious political errors.

However, the general tendency of history has been determined and cannot be changed." (8) The presence of Soviet revisionist social imperialism is a temporary historical detour. But, like capital imperialism, it is weighed down by all sorts of contradictions: The contradiction between the Soviet revisionist bureaucratic monopoly bourgeoisie, on the one hand, and the proletariat and all the laboring people of the Soviet Union, on the other; the contradiction between Soviet revisionist social imperialism and the people of the colonies and the whole world; and the contradiction between Soviet revisionist social imperialism and capital imperialism, especially United States imperialism. All of these are becoming increasingly acute. Because of the existence and development of these contradictions, Soviet revisionist social imperialism will surely be discarded in the museum of history by the people of the Soviet Union and the world. Lenin asserted, 'Imperialism is the eve of socialist revolution." (9) Soviet revisionist social imperialism is the eve of a second socialist October Revolution. Chairman Mao pointed out: "The Soviet Union is a socialist country and the Communist Party of the Soviet Union was created by Lenin. Although the leadership of the Party and government of the Soviet Union is now usurped by revisionists, I would advise our comrades to firmly believe that the broad Soviet people, Party members, and cadres are good people and want revolution. Revisionist rule will not last long." (10) Under the great banner of Leninism and with the support of the people of the world, the Soviet people, who have a glorious revolutionary tradition, will eventually bury Soviet revisionist social capitalism. Their success will once again allow the brilliance of proletarian dictatorship, socialism, and Marxism-Leninism to shine over the land of the Soviet Union.

Let the ruling class tremble before the communist revolution. The proletarians have nothing to lose but their chains. They have a world to win.

Workingmen of all countries, unite! (11)

Major Study References

Lenin, "On the Task of the Third International," Complete Works of Lenin, Vol. 29.

Chairman Mao, "Talk with American Correspondent Anna Louise Strong."

Chairman Mao, "A Congratulatory Telegram to the Fifth Congress of the Labor Party of Albania," October 25, 1966.

Review Problems

1. How does one recognize the nature of Soviet revisionist social imperialism from the basic economic characteristics of imperialism?
2. Why will the rule of the Brezhnev renegade clique in the Soviet Union not be long?

Notes

1) Imperialism, the Highest Stage of Capitalism, Selected Works of Lenin, Vol. 2, Jen-min ch'u-pan-she, 1972, p. 827.

2) "Resolutions on the Present Situation. Seventh National Congressional Conference (April Congressional Conference) of the Social Democratic Labor Party (Bolshevik) of Russia," Complete Works of Lenin, Vol. 24, p. 277.

3) Marx, Critique of the Gotha Program, Selected Works of Marx and Engels, Vol. 3, Jen-min ch'u-pan-she, 1972, p. 17.

4) "On the National Superiority Complex of the Great Russian People," Selected Works of Lenin, Vol. 2, Jen-min ch'u- pan-she, 1972, p. 611.

5) A Talk by Chairman Mao on May 11, 1964. Quoted in Jen-min jih-pao [People's Daily], April 22, 1970.

6) "War and Russia's Social Democratic Party," Complete Works of Lenin, Vol. 21, p. 13.

7) Quoted from Jen-min jih-pao [People's Daily], April 28, 1969.

8) "On Coalition Government," Selected Works of Mao Tse- tung, Vol. 3, Jen-min ch'u-pan-she, 1968, p. 932.

9) "Preface to Imperialism, the Highest Stage of Capital- ism, Selected Works of Lenin, Vol. 2, Jen-min ch'u-pan-she 1972, p. 730.

10) Quoted from Jen-min jih-pao [People's Daily], June 11, 1967.

11) Communist Manifesto, Selected Works of Marx and Engels, Vol. 1, Jen-min ch'u-pan-she, 1972, pp. 285-86.